# Interpreting
# THE
# BIBLE
in
theology and the
church

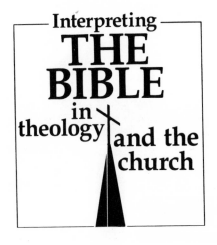

# Interpreting
# THE
# BIBLE
## in
## theology and the
## church

Henry Vander Goot

The Edwin Mellen Press
New York and Toronto

Symposium Series
Volume 11

**Library of Congress Cataloging in Publication Data**

Vander Goot, Henry
    Interpreting the Bible in theology and the church.

    Bibliography: p.
    Includes index.
    1. Bible—Hermeneutics.    I. Title.
BS476.V35   1984      220.6'01       84-9027
ISBN 0-88946-701-3

The Edwin Mellen Press
P.O. Box 450
Lewiston, New York 14092

Cover design: G. Verstraete, Christian Communications Centre

Printed in Canada.

60,070

*To the memory of my parents:*

*Pieter Arjen van der Goot*
*(1909-1982)*
*and*
*Sipkje Walinga-van der Goot*
*(1912-1972)*

# Contents

# Acknowledgements

This project was begun and executed in the Calvin Center for Christian Scholarship, Calvin College. The Calvin Center was established by the Board of Trustees of Calvin College "to promote rigorous, creative, and articulately Christian scholarship which is addressed to the solution of important theoretical and practical issues" (Constitution). The theoretical and practical issue chosen for the year-long research in which I was involved was "Hermeneutics" broadly understood as theories of the interpretation of texts. I have sought to capture the heart of the project in the title of this book by focusing on the problem of interpreting the Bible in the church and the relationship of this interpretation to the "interpretation" of Scripture that takes place in academic theology.

For the opportunity to deal with this important question in theological hermeneutics, I owe a debt of gratitude to Calvin College. It provided me with the free time to participate in the exploration of the chosen topic with six other team members. To the team members who responded extensively in writing and in conversation to my interests and concerns, I also owe a heartfelt word of thanks. The seriousness of the rift between believing Bible use in the church on the one hand and a highly refined but all too often unbelieving deconstruction of the Bible in theology on the other bothered me deeply for the nine years I studied theology in seminary and graduate school. I hope that this small book may be a start on further much needed reflection about this matter.

# Introduction: Stating the Thesis

**The main contention of this essay is that prior to and outside of the scientific study of the Bible in the Christian community of faith, interpretation is already there and that this existing phenomenon of interpretation and immediate confessional response to the Bible is what should fund the theoretical enterprise of theology and biblical studies.** In modern thought an odd reversal has taken place in the order of life and science. Scientific thought is assumed to serve the deconstruction of the world as we phenomenally experience it and put in its place reliable models of reality provided by the various scientific disciplines. In theology this has meant, among other things, that trained experts are expected to interpret Scripture for the community of believers. However, it will be claimed in this essay that theology and the scientific study of the Bible have the responsibility to interpret the interpretations of the life of faith that already exist.

This main claim will be argued in this essay through the consideration of various corollaries that mutually depend on one another and that make the central contention possible. First, there is a fundamental distinction to be made between first and second order forms of knowing; that is, between pre-scientific and scientific thought. Moreover, the former has ordinal precedence over the latter since the life world funds the theoretical enterprise as a whole.

The second corollary concerns the level of interpretation of the Bible to which this essay is addressed, namely the meaning of the Bible as a whole or single structure. That

1

meaning is what I have in mind as the claim is argued that naive Christian apprehensions of faith ought to base the theoretical, theological enterprise. This essay makes no particular claims about how this or that verse in Scripture should be interpreted, or even about the interpretation of this or that chapter of the Bible. It only hopes to contribute to addressing the problem of how the Christian's understanding of the biblical story as a whole is derived and how this in turn relates to the formation of the Christian's scholarly efforts to interpret the Bible. Thus the second corollary concerns specifically the ideas that the meaning of the Bible as a whole is the meaning intended by God, its author, that this meaning is the sense of Scripture immanent in its overall narrative sweep, and that this meaning is minimally the creation-fall-redemption-consummation structure of the biblical narrative. This essay intends to be about that often neglected aspect of biblical interpretation and not about detail questions that might be the concern of biblical studies and exegesis.

The third corollary, not necessarily presented here in the order in which it will be taken up in the essay, is that this overall sense of the biblical story is directly comprehensible to the naive Christian reader. Scientific or critical operations on the text are not required for the story to become formed in the Christian's understanding. The fact that all understanding is mediated and formed does not make it theoretical, abstractive, and methodologically self-conscious. The Christian understanding of the biblical story takes place in the context and tradition of the Christian community of faith and is at once directly and naively grasped.

The fourth corollary is that the overall meaning of biblical Christianity thus directly grasped in the context of the believing community has the right to be considered the real *literal sense* of the *canon*. Literal sense and canonical meaning are terms that have fallen into disrepute after the Reformation. The former has been identified by critics and scholastics alike with the grammatical meaning or the historical reference, or with both. The notion of the literal sense has been identified with the literal*istic* and has thus been discarded. Moreover, "canonical meaning" has been associated with a heavy handed, systematic, doctrinalist, and strained Christological overlay on the scriptural material. Finally, scientism has come to spurn the common sensical and reject it as the false Aristotelian theory of naive realism. The given phenomenal shape and letter of the text have become suspected while the recovery of the real hidden meaning has become the prerogative of an expert class.

On the basis of a hermeneutics of trust and affirmation of the phenomenally given linguistic word, this essay represents a defense of the notions of literal sense and canonical meaning. The literal sense of the biblical storyline is the sense of what Scripture says, which can only be gotten at by way of the method in which Scripture says it. The literal sense is the non-referential, explicative sense of the text of the Bible viewed as a non-fictional, realistic narrative. Moreover, canon is the idea that there is an authoritative whole and that this authoritative whole is the conventional Christian understanding of the Bible's overall message as a creation-fall-restoration-consummation story, which should be the controlling ingredient in the interpretation of the Bible's various parts. Attention to these cardinal notions and terms has slipped out of focus in theology and biblical studies because of the changed framework of understanding in which modern critical hermeneutics works. This essay shall thus consider in what important respects theological hermeneutics differs from models of interpretation that are current in hermeneutical theory generally.

# Chapter I
# Scientific and Pre-Scientific

*"Only as we attend to the direct experience of the biblical text are we able to notice and maintain that the text of Scripture has a unity and integrity of its own. The unity and integrity of the Bible is a function of faith and the function of faith is the primary context within which the truth of the Bible is able to come to expression, setting the framework within which second order study of the text should take place."*

# Chapter I

# Scientific and Pre-Scientific

## Direct Reading

The starting point of biblical and theological hermeneutics is what can be called the "direct" reading of the Bible.[1] This is the experiential phenomenon with which any consideration of biblical interpretation in theology must begin. However with the rise of modern scientific (specifically mathematical) method, which claimed to have discovered a uniform universal substance underlying appearance, a certain methodological dogmatism emerged. This methodologism set itself up *overagainst* what is given to man in naive and direct experience, which modern science came more and more to identify with the Aristotelian theory of naive realism. Yet experience in its fullness underlies every reflective, theoretical act, which is by the nature of the case deliberately partial and aspectual.

In the case of understanding texts, direct reading focuses first on the text itself, just as the movie-goer first simply experiences the movie he is viewing in terms of its full impact. Of course, the reader and movie-goer may subsequently take a second look and focus in on this or that particular side of the experience. Nonetheless, in the order of knowledge the focus on the text and what it says comes first, making subsequent dissection of the whole (ana-lysis) possible. In direct reading one assimilates what the text says (the sense of the text) before one asks what the text meant or what significance it could have.

Moreover, direct, naive reading is aimed at the text as a simple whole. Where deliberate or intentional efforts are not made to bracket this or that and zero in on an object which theoretical thought might set up overagainst itself, the text is experienced in its undivided fullness. The text's "law" and power govern the encounter with its reader.

In the case of Scripture the impact of the whole is not achieved in any one exposure to the Bible. Rather a sense of the whole emerges in the course of ordinary experience in the church, which involves recurrent exposure to the stories of the Bible that as taken together comprise the Bible's single storyline. In addition the meaning of the whole is not necessarily achieved over and over again by every single individual. Nor does the individual reader seem to piece the whole together from the meaning of the Bible's various parts, thus achieving a comprehensive sense of the Christian story. Direct reading is a concept intended to refer to a fundamental level of apprehension that exists within the Christian community in which the reader-believer participates. As K.J. Popma, a prominent Protestant theologian in Holland, has put it: "The naive use of the Bible is characteristic for the congregation."[2] Direct reading thus involves the general problem of the formation of the Christian's understanding of the frame of the story that the Bible gives.

Finally, of signal importance for understanding how the Bible is to be interpreted is the fact that direct reading of the text of the Bible recognizes that the Bible presents the Word of God—God in the sweep of the total story revealing his identity to us.[3] In the direct reading of the Bible as a religious text, it is not read primarily for information about what the ancient Hebrews once believed, nor for information about what was believed in the New Testament church. Moreover, in the naive setting the Bible is not read either as God's Word to the Hebrews or as God's Word to the early church, but as God's revelation to us, the present readers.

Only as we attend to the direct experience of the biblical text are we able to notice and maintain that the text of Scripture has a unity and integrity of its own. The unity and integrity of the Bible is a function of faith and the function of faith is the primary context within which the truth of the Bible is able to come to expression, setting the framework within which second order study of the text should take place. In the direct and full mode of life experience in which all the dimensions of the experience of the Bible are tacitly present, the Bible is experienced as a whole even though it was composed by many human authors speaking out of many different situations. In the full experience of the text this factor of many authors and different contexts of origin necessarily drops out of focus, and so it is not uncritical and naive in the bad sense of the word that in the experience of the believer's use of the Bible the conviction that God is the single author comes basically to determine the reader-believer's point of view. Because this is the structure and character of the believer's ordinary use of and understanding about the Bible, the text of the Bible shows itself to be more than its meanings in the various situations that relate to its composition. As Word of God to us in the present situation the Bible, working with and through history, nonetheless transcends history. As K.J. Popma has argued, attention to the naive sense has to do with "The Divine Word-Revelation as a power breaking through historico-cultural limits and restrictions."[4] In fact that is what becomes prominent (and rightly so) as one observes how the Bible is used in the community of faith.

In summary, we might mention here that the level of meaning to which we refer when emphasizing the meaning of the text as a whole and as God's revelation to us may be designated the text's "canonical sense."[5] Canonical sense, when used to speak of the Bible, refers to the believing community's construal of the Bible as integral, as Word of God to us, and thus as a single standard or rule of faith in the community. Moreover, with respect to this level we also have the most right to speak of the Bible's "literal sense." Literal sense is not the brutely factual sense, the sense as shorn of all of its contextual determinations, but the sense of the parts as determined by the sense of the text as a whole. The literal sense is the sense of the whole that has moreover developed into the conventional understanding in the Christian community of faith.[6]

## A Philosophical Distinction

The above distinction between direct and scientific reflection on which the comments about naive experience are based is related to a distinction evident in much philosophical literature. Phenomenologists like Maurice Merleau-Ponty and Calvin Schrag speak of the difference between lived through experience and scientific reflection.[7] The Dutch philosopher Herman Dooyeweerd has developed extensively the epistemological distinction between ''theoretical and pretheoretical attitudes of thought.''[8] The psychologist Adrian van Kaam develops in depth the distinction between ''reflective and pre-reflective modes of being.''[9] In making these distinctions each of these thinkers has in mind that there are a number of different modes in which we tune ourselves into reality, i.e. in which we experience reality.

The first mode of experience is the *direct* mode. It is the mode in which we relate spontaneously to things (like texts) and persons in the world of our primary experience. In this mode we are *necessarily* related to the world; thus experience in this mode does not include the bending back on reality that is characteristic of *reflection*. Pre-reflective experience is an original and non-contrived way of acting in the world. Being present to the things and persons of our world in this way entails being related to them in their tacitly experienced fullness of being.

The reflective or scientific mode of theoretical thought differs qualitatively from the direct mode. Reflection requires something prior to itself on which reflection takes place and with which it begins. No reflective thought can fund itself. In the theoretical mode a shift of attitude takes place as one bends oneself back on the world of direct experience through which one has lived. In the theoretical mode, the dialectic of subject and object is momentarily intentionally suspended; some one thing or relation or side of things becomes objectified in an intentional act of abstractive thought. A socalled *Gegenstand* relation is established.

In the reflective mode then one focuses one's attention; one takes a second look. In lived-through experience, things are wholes (*Gestalten*) whose many salient features may be grasped at once in a tacit perception of individuality. In the theoretical attitude of thought one focuses abstractively on a thing apart from its context or on an aspect of a thing apart from the whole constellation of relationships that constitute its identity. Scientific, theoretical activity assumes an angle of vision, a view point on the world of lived-through experience. Thus we are able to speak of the various scientific disciplines as each dealing with an *aspect* or *dimension* of things.[10]


## Scientific and Pre-Scientific in Hans-Georg Gadamer

In hermeneutical literature per se this basic distinction between the theoretical and the pre-theoretical has also been prominently operative, especially in the work of Hans-Georg Gadamer. Following in the footsteps of Husserl and Heidegger, Gadamer's major work *Truth and Method* represents a protest against the methodological preoccupations and fixations of modern thought. For Gadamer there is an original truth and there are the various scientific methods and their produce. In all science, whether natural or cultural, there is a necessary objectification and theoretical reduction, according to Gadamer. All science is secondary and derivative because the reality analyzed according to specific rules represents only a small part of the totality of relations. Yet knowledge ratified according to the ideals of modern science is often thought to be the only knowledge of a certain and valid sort.

However, for Gadamer there is "an experience (and knowledge) of truth that transcends the sphere of the control of scientific method . . . ."[11] It is present in conventional wisdom, art, and history. There is a truth antecedent to science that "comes to speech" in these aforementioned pre-scientific modes of experience. *Truth and Method* is presented by Gadamer as an attempt to understand "what the human sciences truly are, beyond their methodological self-consciousness, and what connects them with the totality of our experience of the world."[12]

The view of aesthetic experience and historical knowledge that Gadamer sets forth in *Truth and Method* must then be seen in the context of a critical reflection on methodological dogmatism and the idea that only knowledge established by science is tested and dependable. Though naturally Gadamer concedes a relative legitimacy to rule-governed analysis, Gadamer's central concern is to make vivid the realization that there is a truth "before" that has priority over and funds the sciences. Modern science, Gadamer maintains, has tended oddly to reverse the proper order of the horizon of general experience and theoretical thought.

Much of *Truth and Method* is devoted to a heightening of our awareness of this original truth that is "before" and "beyond" methodological abstraction. In particular Gadamer appeals to the notion of a *sensus communis*, a tradition of accumulated knowledge and insight that constitutes the framework within which human judgment can be correctly applied. But by far the most prominent consideration is given by Gadamer to the experience of art as an horizon of pre-scientific knowledge and truth.[13] Truth is had in the experience of art, according to Gadamer. Accordingly Gadamer expends considerable energy refuting the claims of subjectivistic aestheticisms that separate art and knowledge. Moreover, the full reality of art shows itself according to Gadamer in game or play.[14] In game or play we can take note of a significant model of pre-scientific knowledge for in play the subject is laid hold of by a process in which truth is manifested.

Understanding, according to Gadamer, which is pre- and non-scientific knowledge of truth, means participation in a ground of truth that is "before." This background of truth acquired through life experience in the world is, in Gadamer's terms, "effective history," or tradition.[15] All understanding is borne along by such truth and foreknowledge, and thus all understanding is necessarily borne along and made possible by tradition.

One of the most interesting contributions of Gadamer's work is his subsequent polemic against the so-called "pre-judice against prejudices."[16] Given Gadamer's notion of pre-scientific knowledge, understanding has as one of its conditions "legitimate prejudices."[17] Long before we understand ourselves and the world self-consciously and critically in accordance with the principles of methodical thought, we understand ourselves and the world in a self-evident way. Every moment of understanding takes place within a ground that is already there when the subject of knowledge "comes onto the scene," so to speak. This context of the subject is the subject's tradition, the set of pre-judices in terms of which this or that new object of understanding becomes assimilated. According to Gadamer the longstanding prejudice against prejudice gives rise to the illusion of an absolute reason that creates knowledge *ex nihilo*. However, hermeneutics has the responsibility, according to Gadamer, not to conceal or deny prejudices but to examine our fore-meanings so that we may consciously assimilate them and notice how they are indispensable conditions for the appropriation of what further presents itself to us in the open horizon of our life experience.

Similarly Gadamer rehabilitates the notion of authority.[18] Knowing by authority is not necessarily in con-flict with knowing what is true. According to Gadamer, authority, i.e. that someone else's judgment would take precedence over one's own, is not necessarily opposed to reason and freedom, for someone else's superior knowledge can be a reason for accepting something as being true. Gadamer speaks in this connection of "objective prejudices."[19]

In summary we might say then that Gadamer's work maintains strongly the distinction between pre-scientific and scientific thought, and that the former has ordinal priority over the latter. Moreover, the primary experience of the world includes a notion of the primary experience of texts, which too are part of the world of our immediate experience. In the mode of relating to things in the world in terms of their fullness, our experience is direct, immediate, and non-selfconscious. We need only think of how we ordinarily read books and view movies.

This is, of course, not to say that our naive reading is not subjective, or not formed culturally and historically. There is without doubt a *context* of understanding in the pre-theoretical mode. For example, there are the various communities to which we *nolens volens* belong; that is, there is our intellectual tradition, there is society, there is the cultural heritage of which we are a part and the specific social groupings of which we are members. All of these factors make us what we are specifically and concretely. Yet in the pre-scientific mode of experience we understand ourselves and the things that surround us in a self-evident way since we are not conscious of the forces that environ us and in terms of which we are enabled to know and to understand. At best we can become conscious of them after knowing has occurred and we reflect back on it. But then we are already implicated in this context of knowing. When we are tuned into texts in the fullness of their being, we think and understand spontaneously in the terms of our life context or tradition. Not only is tradition inevitable and good, our tradition becomes our second nature.

This is the point of Gadamer's *real* contribution in *Truth and Method* to hermeneutics. Subjectivity is inevitable. Moreoever, subjectivity is not necessarily limiting or a deficiency. The *tabula rasa* of objectivity is not only impossible, but not even a desirable goal. In addition, we learn from Gadamer that subjectivity is itself formable.

The context of the human subject is history and tradition, and these are themselves cultural and human products. Finally, from Gadamer we see that it is not the case that any subjectivity is as good as the next (cultural relativism or historicism). The question of what an appropriate subjectivity might be, given a certain goal of knowledge and understanding, does greater justice to the question of truth and its discovery than the notion of a contextless human subject, which is illusory and even undesirable.

It is in this sense that I wish to employ the notion of naive experience and the hermeneutically relevant idea of a naive, first order, and direct reading of the biblical text: (1) the Bible is read most appropriately in a life context; (2) the Bible is read most apropos to its nature in a life context that has itself been formed and informed by the Bible. That reading is most full and direct which itself takes place under the power of the Bible's Word. Moreover, coming under the power of the Bible's Word is primary and it is this that takes place only in the believing community in trusting intercourse with Scripture. Finally, such a relationship with the Bible must be presupposed in any second order, scientific investigation of it that strives to avoid violating its object. It is indeed questionable whether most modern scientific study of the Bible in the so-called critical, post-Enlightenment period rests on such a necessary and appropriate pre-scientific base.

To be sure, the specific context or tradition of understanding that Gadamer has in mind in his work is the European or Germanic tradition of western culture and *Ausbildung*. In my essay, however, that cultural "community" or "tradition" could not qualify, from a normative point of view, as the context of Christian understanding, even though the history of western culture is intimately bound up with the history and tradition of the Christian community of faith. In this essay I have spoken of "believing reading" and of the Christian community of faith as the framework within which direct reading of Scripture ought to take place for the truth of Scripture to come to expression. Here the context of understanding is defined by the community of those who appropriate Scripture in obedient and believing affirmation of it, and, hence, by the tradition of Christian orthodoxy, which has come to its most normative expression in the ecumenical confessions of the early church.[20]

Last but not least, tradition and culture ought not to be viewed merely as the historical accumulation of human products, as Gadamer tends to do. The context of man is more than what man freely brings into being through his shaping of culture and history, i.e. it is more than a sheer human product, decision, or form of self-expression. Culture and history are products of man's *response* to a "law" of God for culture and history—what in traditional Christian theology is called "the order of creation," or "the civil use of the law."[21] In culture and history too there continues to be a sovereign expression of the life of the created order.[22] Hence, the context of the human subject is also that world of creation to which man must be responsible in his discharge of the cultural mandate "to be fruitful, to multiply, to replenish the earth, to subdue it and have dominion over it" (Genesis 1:28). The general revelation of God and his will in creation—which it takes Scripture for man properly to grasp—is also there at the base of human culture and tradition, and this revelation and world cannot be coerced or ignored by man.

Though Gadamer hints at this conception of world as the context of man, he either does not make enough of it or he does not conceive it properly. He admits that we live in a state of "constant overstimulation of our historical consciousness."[23] Moreover, Gadamer's lengthy analysis of the notion of a *sensus communis* too is reminiscent of some notion that there is law in the universe and that it obtains also for culture and history to such an extent that we can speak of *common* sense and *common* human notions that relate to a *common* world of creation that all men share.[24]

Yet, here too Gadamer's formulation is subjectivistic, tending toward the notion that knowledge of that order of God for creation is given immediately or naturally within human consciousness. Finally, Gadamer stresses that texts open us up to the world but not enough beyond the notions of tradition and prejudices is said about what that world is essentially to which all culture and history are human response. However such a more fundamental, ontological view of the world context of the human subject is, it seems to me, required by an adequate hermeneutic of naive experience.

# Chapter II
# The Bible as Narrative

> *"Not only are there narratives in the Bible . . . ; the Bible itself is overall best described as a narrative. We not only have the various books of the Bible but the Bible itself as a book. As Augustine shows in his* The City of God, *the Bible itself narrates a history of mankind from creation to consummation. As a whole the Bible consists of a single, ongoing composite narrative. It is a universal history, an apocalyptic story."*

# Chapter II
# The Bible as Narrative

Narrative is the linguistic form appropriate to the pre-reflective life of the Christian community of faith.[1] What the community's convictions are come to written expression first in symbolic and imagistic form. The symbols and images of religious communities are not reflectively produced. Moreover, the activities of conceptualization and definition draw on the community's accepted images and thus come later, at least logically, if not also temporally.

In the case of the Bible too there is an abundance of narrative material. There are stories and narrations that are either historical in a relatively close use of that term, or stories that evidence a history-like character.[2] These stories have a narrator, recount interactions between characters and circumstances, are constructed along a storyline, and have the purpose of identifying an agent, namely God.

Moreover, these narratives are generally presented as realistic portrayals of life. As Hans Frei has said: "Much of the Bible consists of realistic narration . . . ."[3] The stories take for granted that what is depicted in them happened the way that it is depicted, however extraordinary to the reader the events may appear to be. The stories of the Bible are presented as intimately connected with the world of mundane reality. By realism is thus meant that the meaning of a text is the "text's depiction," which provides a "straightforward appreciation of the narrative features of the biblical stories in their own right."[4]

Moreover, in Scripture the narrative places the events recorded and personages described in the sequence of ordinary history. Events and persons are most emphatically not presented as having their significance outside of the ordinary course of events in the work-a-day world. These recorded events do not say one thing and mean something quite different, abstract, and ideal. In fact they are given exactly in a way that underscores how they themselves are the real meaning of all that has transpired.

To put it in more theoretical terms, meaning and reference are kept tightly together. No theoretical structure or general framework needs to be brought to the narrative to explicate its meaning. In fact the narrative is presented even to govern later theoretical formations. The narrative itself as ordinarily given history is central and the point of reference. It intends to be about reality and resists the separation of its meaning from its form and from the way in which it says what it says.[5] Realistic narrative itself represents the most fundamental reality.

Not only are there narratives in the Bible however; the Bible itself is overall best described as a narrative.[6] We not only have the various books of the Bible but the Bible itself as a book. As Augustine shows in his *The City of God*, the Bible itself narrates a history of mankind from creation to consummation. As a whole the Bible consists of a single, ongoing, composite narrative. It is a universal history, an apocalyptic story. As Charles Wood has said:

> When one regards the biblical canon as a whole, the centrality to it of a narrative element is difficult to overlook: not only the chronological sweep of the whole, from creation to new creation, including the various events and developments of what has sometimes been called "salvation history," but also the way the large narrative portions interweave and provide a context for the remaining materials so that they, too, have a place in the ongoing story, while these other materials—parables, hymns, prayers, summaries, theological expositions—serve in different ways to enable readers to get hold of the story and to live their way into it.[7]

Moreover, when we read the Bible directly as canon and attend to the Bible's overall story, we naturally construe it in a certain way. For instance, the narrative is presented as the Word of God and we perceive it accordingly as a sacred text that has God as its author. In the situation of ordinary use the Bible is taken to be by God and about God and how he relates himself to his people. In addition, in the phenomenon of believing reading and use of the Bible, the believing community reads the Bible as God's address to us in the present situation. Furthermore, in the situation of ordinary use the Bible is rightly read as a story about the beginning, middle, and end of life, of our personal lives and of the life of the cosmos itself. The pattern of beginning-middle-end presents what is in effect a Christian view of history, within which everything that transpires is located and in terms of which alone everything makes ultimate sense.

From observation of how the Bible is read and used in the life of the believing community, we see that the composite narrative shape of the canon is what stands out, attuning the reader to the concordance of the Bible's various parts. In the accepting and non-critical attitude, an overall sense of harmony prevails. The text of the Bible as we now have it and ordinarily use it in the religious community brings about a focus on its unity as God's story about the history of the world and the reader's personal history as this fits into the bigger picture. With this focus we read the Bible as universal history, seeing how it places the sequence of ordinary chronology within its events. The Bible takes with ultimate seriousness the intimate interrelationship of the divine and the human, of what it calls "heaven and earth." A separate history of special divine events (*Heilsgeschichte* or metastory) as contrasted with the mundane and ordinary could not possibly have the same impact.

In addition, when we read the Bible as a narrative, we become sensitive to the importance of the Bible's arrangement of events (for example, creation first, redemption later) and books (Old Testament followed by New) and thus also to the primacy of the final redaction.[8] This arrangement bears heavily on the proper interpretation of the Bible.[9] In the naive and direct attitude of thought, interpretation of the Bible's parts is determined by the text of the Bible as we now have it. The sense of the text is essentially not to be established by some putative extratextual situation or intentions of the human authors to which research claims to have access outside of and beyond what the text itself offers. Form and content belong together. In the full and believing mode of Scripture use, the Bible is read for what it itself claims to be, i.e. the Word of God. Hence, in the naive and full mode it is read from the point of view of its content, i.e. from the point of view of God and his acts, not primarily from the point of view of its recipients and their beliefs about God and his acts. In faith we insist that the historical and cultural point of view is not to be considered the rationally certain one in comparison to the perspective of faith, which is often wrongly considered a matter of private opinion and pure choice. Even for the scientific study of the Bible what is central, determining the content of the Bible, is that the Bible's events are presented from the high ground from which they address us. Because we have the Bible we assume, and rightly so, that we are privileged to know God's deeds *from his vantage point.*[10]

If we then follow the narrative order, we see that creation is the presupposition of the fall story, and the creation and fall stories together are the presupposition of the history of salvation. Finally in the Bible the last things are interpreted primarily in continuity with the first, as already the early church affirmed with its formula that "the last things repeat the first."[11] Though creation "grows up," to use the language of Irenaeus, in salvation an effort is made to return to the original spiritual tendency of creation that characterized all things in the state of rectitude.

The form, then, of the Bible's arrangement of narratives suggests strongly that the fundamental theme of the biblical revelation is the restoration of fallen existence to its original right direction. The biblical storyline is a creation-fall-redemption-consummation one. This is the shape of the story as a whole on the face of it, apprehended thus in the mode of faith because it is the direct appearance of what is there. This order and arrangement is what strikes one first as one is still trying to ascertain what the text is claiming.

However, as Augustine already well knew, that order of the narrative in the Bible as we now have it changes, depending on one's perspective. For example, from the perspective of the *recipient* of the things of God, Jesus Christ and faith come first, while it is through him that we come to know the Father Creator by faith. In the order or logic of faith itself—which is the order of the text as such—creation is first, redemption follows. But in the order of *our coming to faith*, Jesus Christ and redemption become the point from which the believer moves outward toward creation and consummation. With secularism has come the anthropocentristic assumption that everything outside of man must justify its existence to him (*cogito, ergo sum*). When this conception of the ground of certainty took hold of modern thought, the push toward a Christocentric view of the "real, underlying" structure of biblical narrative became strong in theology, as we see clearly already in the great Schleiermacher. The given narrative shape of the Bible became demeaned as appearance, naive objectifying thinking, or as the mistaken arrangement of naive final redactors. It is this historical-critical perspective on the present shape of the Bible that the community of faith and the naive reader rightly and instinctively resist.

Finally, reading the Bible directly as narrative helps us to come to a proper apprehension of the non-narrative discourse of the Bible.[12] We have already noted that the Bible as a whole has a narrative structure even though its various parts consist of both narrative and non-narrative elements. Although we have argued that the whole Bible has the character of its narrative parts, we should not neglect to attend to how the non-narrative parts fit into the whole. Moreover, as we attend to this dimension, we can see how the narrative of the Bible as a whole is related to extra-biblical, non-narrative discourse about what's in the Bible. What is the right way in which the narrative of the Bible as a whole is provided with intelligibility?

First we would note the unbreakable link between law and the narrative of creation in the Bible.[13] The Torah is introduced by the work of creation. Law thus is a non-narrative commentary on the narrative of creation in the Bible. Law refers to the enduring element in creation, to that structure of order and discipline within which the life of obedience as well as disobedience makes sense in the Bible. Law tells us what kind of life the world within which the characters of the narrative are placed sustains. Furthermore, wisdom in the Bible might also be viewed as primarily related to Scripture's creation narrative. As Walter Zimmerli has said, "Wisdom thinks resolutely within the framework of a theology of Creation."[14] Wisdom sayings explore the world's elements of perpetuity, showing how the wise man finds his proper way in and with the world. Moreover, the Psalms reenact, frequently in the cultic situation, the narratives of the Old Testament for purposes of praise, lamentation and penitence. Finally, in the New Testament the epistles serve as commentaries on the Gospels, the narratives of Christ's life and redemption.[15]

Already then within the Bible we can take note of the important linkage between narrative and non-narrative modes of discourse. The function of these non-narrative modes seems to be to provide the narratives with intelligibility. Paul Ricoeur has suggested that within Scripture itself there is a movement from narrative to images to paradigms and finally on into theology itself.[16] Inasmuch as this movement takes place within the Bible, the Bible takes up into its form as a *single* narrative the means for its own overall intelligibility.

In fact there is a certain inevitable interpretation created by the force of the events recorded. The events have a power and are best appropriated by those immediately affected. Because the events and their immediate "interpretation" are inseparable in the Bible, the two together become what is interpreted by the reader of the biblical text. In the Bible God's works and the response to them of their recipients comprise the one revelation of the Word of God. The historical-critical distinction between what really happened on the one hand and the mythologizing interpretation of those events by Israel and the New Testament community on the other seems irreconcilable with a conventionally Christian doctrine of Scripture as revelation.

A last comment is in order at this point about the relationship between narrative and extra-biblical, non-narrative discourse about what's in the Bible. Most generally we refer to such extra-biblical, non-narrative discourse as Christian systematic theology. If the Bible were only a collection of stories, there could be no coherent grasp of the Bible as a single book. But direct reading has roots in and expresses the coherent story of the Bible; moreover, theology has roots in this first order grasp of the whole. Theology, summaries, confessional formulas, and credos all serve to remind us that the Bible is a single, ongoing, cumulative narrative and thus can be viewed as a canonical unity.

# Chapter III

# The Priority and Sovereignty of the Text of Scripture

> *"As the reader (of Scripture) imbibes the spirit and mind that informs the text and that is by God's decree available to man in the Bible, he is changed; the strange world of the Bible becomes his and he now goes about trying to make the world of his life relevant to the new world that he has discovered and that has compelled him to accept it at the deepest level of his existence. It is in this way that man is transformed and controlled by the Word of God.* The revelation of the Word of God becomes his context."

# Chapter III

# The Priority and Sovereignty of the Text of Scripture

In modern hermeneutical theory much attention has been paid to the connection between texts and what accompanies them. Those accompanying contexts are essentially reducible to authors, who originate texts, or to readers, who use them and construe them in certain ways. Modern thought has been excessively overstimulated by these ideas, which have even trickled down to the high school level.

Naturally there is no reason to deny or ignore these relationships in knowledge that we derive from texts. It is unnecessary, for example, to deny that the Bible is interpreted by the community in which it is read and in which it is taken to authorize and warrant certain actions.[1] In the Christian community of faith there are practices, confessions, and even institutions that are the immediate context within which the text of the Bible gets read and appropriated. The crucial questions, however, are (1) whether historical particularity and conditionedness are essentially *limitations*, making all knowledge tentative and provisional, and (2) what the exact connection is between what's in the Bible and what's outside of it in the Christian community that uses the Bible. How is the meaning of what's in the text of the Bible related to the way in which the Bible functions within the community of faith?

The debate over this question is one of long standing. We are all familiar with the Scripture *and* Tradition dictum of classical Catholicism.[2] More recently—probably because of our heightened consciousness of the subject-reader's contribution to the discernment of meaning—a meaning-is-use dictum has emerged in theological literature. Especially David Kelsey's *The Uses of Scripture in Recent Theology* advances a functionalist view of Scripture. Kelsey comes extremely close to the conclusion that meaning is established by the praxis of the Bible's users, which are the various irreducibly diverse theological and confessional communities.[3]

There is no reason to deny that the reading of Scripture takes place within a context and that that has signal implications for what readers see in the Bible. Surely that fact alone, since it is inevitable, does not jeopardize the possibility of knowledge of what's in the text. That all knowledge is personal, particular, and context-dependent need not be regarded as a *qualification* of the claim that there can be knowledge of what's in a text, or even that there are texts that have a content and internal identity. The crucial question is whether the context of knowledge is viewed as an autonomous or independent horizon of meaning alongside that of the text of the Bible.

In relation to that question the traditional Protestant argument has been that at the fundamental level the only way to maintain the sovereignty of God in the matter of his knowability is to prefer a view of the text of Scripture as sovereign. In the case of scriptural revelation at the level of the question about authority, it is not possible to maintain a dialectic of the two horizons of text and readers. When all is said and done, Protestant Christianity prefers a focus first on the text of the Bible with its claim that the internal sense of the text has priority over any other.[4] The meaning of the biblical text must be sought in the light of the horizon of its internal structure to protect as best as possible against the accommodation of the text to the wrong prejudices of the reader. At the fundamental, religious level text and reader are not mutually corrective and interdependent, as general hermeneutical theory would insist is always the case. Furthermore, in the discussion to follow of the relationship of Scripture to the context of the reader (what I shall call "creation," or "experience"), this Protestant preference for an internal view of meaning in the Bible can be defended rationally as taking into account the idea that all reading is necessarily context-dependent.

## Scripture and creation

Traditionally the major form in which the question of Scripture's relationship to the world of its reader has been raised in Christian theology is the question of the relationship between "natural knowledge" coming from experience on the one hand and revelation derived from Scripture on the other. The first point to be made in connection with this distinction is that Scripture and creation (the actual world and its history) belong inextricably together. We do not here yet touch on the important question of the priority of the one over the other and the exact nature of that priority. Here we want simply to say that Scripture and creation are correlative. To isolate the one from the other is inappropriate, for the effort to cut them loose from one another leads to a distortion of both the one apparently exclusively used and the one erroneously eclipsed from the discussion.[5]

Hence, it is inappropriate to allege that experience is a source of the knowledge of God and that Scripture is yet another or additional one.[6] The notion of two so-called "books" of revelation (nature and Scripture) is misleading, for so to describe the terms is to miss the character of the inseparable mutual relationship that these two sustain to one another. Experience, the world of the reader in the case of the interpretation of Scripture, is not a source of the knowledge of God *alongside of* the occurrence of revelation in Scripture. Neither is Scripture a substitute for nor alternative to the world and experience. There is only *one* revelation and there is no revelation at all for us apart from experience and Scripture as taken together in their bipolar impact.

Moreover, we must see that these two, experience and Scripture, are magnitudes of a signally different order or kind. Thus they can neither substitute for one another nor each contribute in the same way to a joint product. On the one hand, experience is first and foremost experience of *creation*, experience of that structure of order and law within which we have been placed by our Creator. It is the world of facts, realities, objects, persons and entities. It is the orderly arrangement of things. Scripture is, on the other hand, primarily that *by which* we make our way *in* the world of experience. Though Scripture depicts the world and is even in a lingual sense a piece of the world, it is not the world of experience itself, or at least it can be no alternative to experience in the world. Scripture is rather a direction-giving guide for life in the world—the only right one, as a matter of fact, in a fallen world. It is not *what* there is to see, but that *by which* we see.[7] And so in hermeneutics we cannot say "Scripture alone" and mean by this something that well-nigh eclipses the reader, his context, and the world of experience out of which he comes to the text of the Bible.

## Scripture and Fall

The very fact, however, that we would separate Scripture and experience (special and general revelation) as we often do reflects that we live in a broken world. It is not just the case that Scripture and experience are by kind (ontologically speaking) two distinguishable magnitudes that perform signally different, though mutually interdependent, functions. That fact we have already stressed. But it is also the case that we do not view Scripture, a special divine presence and word, as a perfectly natural or normal aspect of things that everyone in general needs.

Because of the disruption of our existence, experience has, so to speak, imagined it possible to go its own way.

The secular fiction has emerged that experience is self-explanatory, a light unto itself, and that the principle of its proper self-positioning is inherent within itself. One might refer most properly to the situation in which it is natural and normal to depend on a personal word or "special" revelation from God the original creational situation before the fall. One would thus accordingly refer to the situation in which such dependence were considered special, abnormal, or only for some, as the fallen or sinful situation (our present experience). Hence arises the problem of experience *and* Scripture, as if the two were not together originally.

What we must never forget then is that so-called special and general revelation belong together, that they were once one, and that, though distinguishable, they are not separable. In the lapsarian state, it is indeed unfortunately the case that the one revelation of God has become experienced as twofold, general and special, whereas before the fall the special or particular and the general were one. We ought never to view the special as having been added later because of sin. Rather the special and the general got broken apart and dissociated because of sin. Whereas in the beginning the special was really *for all*, after the fall the special became the way into the general *only for those who believe*. (For those who did and do not believe, pseudo special revelational ways of conceiving general revelation were and are fabricated, as Calvin argues incisively in the first five chapters of his *Institutes of the Christian Religion*.) In other words, to think about the world in what we now regard as specifically Christian terms was once, before the fall, perfectly natural, normal, and universally the case. Now, in the lapsarian situation, it is in fact abnormal that special revelation (the particularly "Christian") has become separated from the generally human, becoming, in the minds of many Christians as well as non-Christians, only the Christian community's way of talking about the common reality all men share.

We should note thus that from a Christian and biblical point of view, special revelation is not to be understood as one culturally limited and particular expression of the one revelation of God all men, Christian and non-Christian alike, share; as if Christians have *their* way into God's universal revelation and non-Christians their equally valid, alternative avenue. According to Scripture, there is only one special revelation that befits the general revelation of God in creation. Scripture is the norm, the special or particular revelation by which every other alleged "special revelation" must be evaluated.

From this we see too that the very formulation of our problem in terms of Scripture *and* experience betokens that experience is itself disrupted. Experience rightly lived according to the original order of creation includes, as one of its natural aspects, the principle of special revelation. The fact that some live by the illusion that the principle of special revelation is dispensable is itself a consequence of the fall. Moreover, it is to this abnormal spiritual tendency towards autonomy that Scripture is addressed after the fall as a redemptive remedy. Scripture is now also useful and necessary to change our position and to transform our feeling-perception (*Weltanschauung*) of the whole. Scripture is not new things, but a new view on things.

As we turn to the matter of the priority of Scripture over experience, we mean to be addressing the epistemological question of man's view of himself and his place within the world. We do not mean to suggest that the Bible can provide everything. For example, we do not mean to promote the idea that the Bible both reorients man and that it provides him with a short cut to the norms and laws of the world. When later in this essay we advocate an "incorporation of the world of the reader into the world of the Bible," we have in mind specifically this crucial point: that the perspective with which man is to live in the world and thus the perspective by which he is to read and study Scripture itself may not be established independent of, or even only in dialectical relationship with, the world that the Bible envisions for him. Any other view that goes beyond this of how the Bible "provides a world" and gives us special advantages such that we do not really have to go about the normal processes of norm-discerning in life runs Gnostic dangers that are strictly to be avoided.[8]

## Scripture and Church

Thus far we have spoken of Scripture and creation, or Scripture and experience, and have assumed that creation is fallen and that mankind is fallen humanity. Experience thus needs to be restored; humanity's disrupted existence must be turned around again. Now the experience of fallen humanity restored is the church, which is the life of the people of God as intended in the original creation[9] And so, as we stress the correlativity of Scripture and experience and consider the Bible in the life of the Christian community, we are faced with the problem of Scripture and the church. Scripture and the church too belong indissolubly together. That is the form of our problem as we consider the normal, i.e., normative, situation of the Bible in a context that has itself been (or at least is open to be) formed by the Bible.

As we then turn to this question of the relationship of Scripture and the Christian community, we are confronted with the problem of Scripture and its relationship to what is outside of Scripture in the form most relevant for understanding how Scripture ought to be read. The church originates practices, confessions, and even institutions that constitute the context within which the Bible is appropriated. There is a normal Christian process of working out of the Bible, of going beyond the Bible into the world of life experience. The world of ecclesial experience brought about in this way is the horizon out of which the believing reader of the Bible comes to the Bible with an already in-position world of expectations and questions, a fact that is not only inevitable but perfectly normal and affirmable as well.

However, at the fundamental religious level that process of interaction between the Bible and its believing reader is not really a give and take process at all. The Word of God in the Bible is not just an opinion that has to be taken into consideration. Simply by virtue of the fact that it is a Word that comes *from God*, the Word in the Bible is *Law*-Word.[10] It does not present a possibility but issues a demand. Moreover, the situation of the reader is not the situation of considering options but the situation of subjection. The reader is asked to do more than fit bits and pieces of the Bible's world into his own already intact world. Where Scripture leads, the reader must be ready to dismantle the already-in-position world of his own. That to which he must be open is more than what is analogous to anything that is already a part of his life experience. In short, the reader must be ready to let his own previous world, including his own previous world view, be taken over by the world-transforming world view of the Bible.

In reverent reading there should be no possibility to form Scripture by any question or assumption about its reader's own existential situation. We do not have to provide the Bible with a question or a framework for it to be interpreted rightly. So-called formal tools—such as philosophy—describing the existential situation of man, or reader assumptions about his own situation outside of the text of the Bible are, rather, to be held in suspension; for any possibility of forming the Word in Scripture by assumptions even about the reader himself would constitute a threat to the sovereignty and authority of biblical revelation. In the situation of reverent reading no opportunity is given to make assumptions about the man who listens *because Scripture contains and provides its own.*

Where Scripture is read and heard (the only other option being actively to ignore its claim), and hence, where a meeting occurs between Scripture and the reader, the message that is in Scripture is acknowledged as appropriate to the existential situation of man. This is what it means to have faith, or to believe. In other words, the message qua message brings with itself its own assumptions about what is "outside." The Bible is both a message and a framework. In reverent reading, as Scripture makes its entrance, Scripture's own assumptions about the world and man's situation in it should become the reader's own assumptions about himself, about creation and the predicament of man. The only authentic entrance into the gospel of redemption in Scripture is the protological assumption of Scripture itself that "creation and sin, taken together, describe the human situation."[11]

It is for this reason that I would also contend that at the fundamental level, we do not go to the Bible to do *inquiry*. Inquire is what we do of nature, or of ordinary texts. With respect to ordinary texts we take the stance of inquiry; there gets established an intentional subject-object relationship of theoretical thought. We come with our questions and search the Scriptures for evidence that might cast light on what the answers should be. We thus self-position ourselves in relation to Scripture, but the question is whether such antecedent self-positioning is acceptable from the point of view of Scripture itself.

I would contend that we ought not to view our use of Scripture as a coming to Scripture with our own questions. Reverent reading is "listening in." When we ordinarily confront a text, a written discourse, there is dialogue between the text and the reader. There is a give and take relation because the text is out of another time and place. The meaning is not self-evident and so through the dialogue of text and reader the meaning comes gradually to emerge. This is so because the time of the text is not our time; because there is distantiation rather than identification and participation. Our time does not exhaust or encompass the time of the text nor does the time of the text include us and our time.

At the religious level, the picture and situation is quite different in the case of the Bible. The Bible is the revelation of the Word of God. Even our general categories of understanding, such as the subject-object relationship, or the dialectic of subject and object, require revision in light of the radicality of the notion of revelation. As Dietrich Bonhoeffer argues: "In principle, the idea of a contingent revelation of God in Christ denies the possibility of the I's self-comprehension outside of the reference to revelation."[12] Even our commonplace philosophical ways of thinking about things need to be shaped by the idea of revelation. To ignore this is both to fail to understand the pseudo-revelatory foundations of much secular philosophy and to resist a thorough-going and intrinsicist integration of faith and knowledge. Bonhoeffer's call to unify the aims of even epistemology and true ontology within an "ecclesiastical thought" ought to be heeded.[13]

In connection with the question of our relationship to Scripture, we would contend accordingly that the notion of a dialogue or dialectic between the horizon of the reader and the horizon of the text proves not to be an incisive enough analysis of interpreting the Bible. At the fundamental religious level at which we consider man's existential confrontation with the revelation of God in Scripture, this model falls short. In the case of our relation to Scripture, dialogue, the mutual give and take of subject and object, is *not* the prominent feature of the meeting. In fact all such rhetoric about the connection works against the radicality of the idea of revelation itself. As Kornelis Miskotte has said: "Somewhere man must definitely submit if he wishes to arrive at more than a psychological fact."[14] When the hearer-reader of the Bible listens to the Bible, he is really "listening in" because the world and time of the Bible are so extensive that they include all times and places and thus *in faith* also the time and place of the reader. There is therefore no dialogue, no multiplicity of horizons, because in faith there is no real distantiation. In faith the horizon of the text *is* the horizon of the reader.

Finally, in the view just presented the priority and authority of Scripture over church is implied. Viewed in terms of this priority, the history of the church, of the people of God in the world of creation, is the history of the "interpretation" of the Bible.[15] Church tradition is important because church tradition, where it is what it ought to be, is the Christian community's elaboration of the Bible *in concreto*. Though the Christian tradition is, of course, not itself the Bible, it can be biblical, i.e. informed by the Bible; and so it can be the tradition of experience within which the Bible has been made applicable. Tradition thus understood, we would contend, far from vitiating the principle of *sola scriptura*, is the actual means by which it is most powerfully vindicated.

## Scripture and Spirit

It is important to ask how in direct reading the Bible exercises its priority, how the Bible subjects its believing reader to itself and becomes the context of assumptions out of which the reader makes use of the Bible.

A partial answer to this question may be attempted by way of an example. It is a common experience in the reading of a novel that the reader becomes taken in by the subject-matter of the book. The author writes with such conviction and compelling presentation that the reader is drawn into its world. It is not uncommon, for example, that the reader of a Sartre novel experiences existentialist depression and extreme cynicism about the world. The novel exudes such power that the reader almost unwittingly imagines himself within the fictional world that it portrays. A process of identification is thus initiated so that the reader forms a bond with some character in the book or with any one of Sartre's many spokesmen. The reader, we might say, has been introduced to Sartre's world and comes to experience imaginatively what it is like to participate in that world.

Even when the reader puts down his book and resumes other life activities, he may not be able to shrug off the impact of Sartre's novel. Not only has his reading experience been a unique one; his entire life-orientation has been influenced in a significant way. The result may even be that the reader comes to identify himself as an existentialist person—a not too unrealistic possibility if he continues to read and be moved by Sartre's upsetting stories. The reader indeed comes away from the reading experience with a new disposition to life that has further impact upon his experience even of things quite unrelated to the reading of books. The reader's experience will have thus taken on a new quality, whether it be judged good or bad.

Though the Bible's vision of the world is authoritative and thus confronts its reader with a demand rather than an option, *how* the Bible subjects its reader is similar to how the sympathetic reader of a Sartre novel becomes taken in. When the reader of Scripture is led by the Bible he is drawn into its world and into its mentality. (I am speaking of the believer's first order, direct relation to Scripture.) Through his growing familiarity with the text he comes to identify with its characters and live into their world, which now becomes the model for his world. Even as these characters in the Bible were moved by the Spirit—or hardened their hearts to him—so too the reader is moved by the same Spirit.[16] As he is thus overpowered by the world of the Bible—which often forms a sharp contrast to the world to which he has become accustomed—he is transformed; his mind is renewed, his sensibilities are deepened and hallowed. As the reader imbibes the spirit and mind that informs the text and that is by God's decree available to man in the Bible, he is changed; the strange world of the Bible becomes his and he now goes about trying to make the world of his life relevant to the new world that he has discovered and that has compelled him to accept it at the deepest level of his existence.[17] It is in this way that man is transformed and controlled by the Word of God. *The revelation of the Word of God becomes his context.*

John Calvin uses the image of spectacles as a simile about Scripture. This simile, like the Bible's own image of itself as a light upon our path, is indicative primarily of the spiritual renewal of the heart. The Bible's truth is not just a truth that believers possess and over which they have disposal but is a truth that predisposes them to proper doing. When the whole man is overpowered by the Holy Spirit of God through Scripture, he "begins to work out his own salvation with fear and trembling" (Phil. 2:12b). Even the articulation of belief must be governed by that inner renewal of the person. Therefore, our notion of the regulatory function that Scripture performs, even in our reflection on Scripture itself, must begin with the reality of this total and centrally religious renewal. The Bible must be interpreted by the same "mind" that was created by the force of the Word when the events it relates first transpired.

There is, then, a principal feeling instilled by the Word of God that is immediate, simple and directed to the totality of meaning.[18] This felt-wholeness is the effect upon us of the Word of God which provides for the "perceiver" a total context of perception, a habit pattern of thought and action. The revelation of God creates within us an "affection," so to speak.[19] In the Christian religious experience the perceiver comes to identify with the reality perceived; a participation in that reality is initiated. A position is now occupied *within the whole* and a context of meaning is provided (given!) that shapes the manifold of particular experiences. The believer is under the power of the Word of God.

In referring to this principal experience the Dutch Calvinist philosopher Herman Dooyeweerd employs the metaphor of "knowledge" rather than of "sense" or "feeling." Dooyeweerd emphasizes that the biblical story-line, creation-fall-redemption, is a "motive power," a meaning-laden *principium*, not just an article of faith of which Christians have a theological knowledge. As a "central motive power," creation-fall-redemption is not simply knowledge, in the ordinary sense, but *the key* to true knowledge, which is "neither of a dogmatic-theological, nor of a philosophical nature, but (has) an absolutely central religious significance." By the Holy Spirit, who works through Scripture, this power impinges on us, places us in its grip, and thus becomes "operative in the religious center of our consciousness and existence."[21] The claim of the self to independence is broken not simply where its dependence on necessary presuppositions, control beliefs, or biblical principles is made clear but where even reason itself is set in the context of the central religious sphere of human life.

# The Priority of the Literal Sense and Its Eclipse in Modern Hermeneutics

*"Arguing that the conflation of the literal sense with the original meaning is fatal to the study of the Bible, Charles Wood has sought to call attention to another concept of the literal sense. For pre-critical exegesis, Wood and many others have contended, the literal sense is the meaning intended by God, which is comprehensible to the reader who participates in the community of faith and which requires no critical operations on the text to determine . . .*

*"Without this framework of Christian understanding, Wood argues, the obvious sense becomes opaque. A major thesis of Wood's book is thus that philosophical and critical hermeneutics have become the framework of understanding of the Bible and that therefore the notion of literal sense has itself fallen into disrepute. Shifting attention to the engendering experience outside the text, modern historical criticism has lost interest in the literal sense as understood by pre-critical exegesis, and thus also of the role of the community of faith in the interpretation of Scripture."*

**Chapter IV**

# The Priority of the Literal Sense and Its Eclipse in Modern Hermeneutics

The preceding discussions concerned the phenomenon of direct, full, and naive reading of Scripture in the community of faith as well as the priority of Scripture over experience and tradition in the communication of revelation. These discussions lead directly to a pre-theoretical and intratextual view of meaning in the Bible. On the side of the human subject who reads believingly, we have emphasized the notion of a direct and full reading of the biblical text as a whole. On the side of the text we are inclined to emphasize the importance of the notions of literal sense and narrative depiction. Only stress on these notions can vindicate adequately the ideas of the sovereignty of God and the authority of biblical revelation. The sovereignty of God in the event of making himself known implies the sovereignty of the text of the Bible. The Bible is a standard against which the horizon of the reader must be normed. To do justice to this, it is necessary to maintain that the Bible has a content or internal identity, the discernment of which is not dependent on the application to Scripture of critical operations.

It is the purpose of what follows to elaborate further the idea of the sovereignty of the biblical text and the priority of the literal sense in Scripture. To understand these notions more fully, it is necessary to consider how emphasis on the literal sense, narrative depiction, direct reading, and what it produces have fallen into disrepute in modern critical hermeneutical literature. It is also helpful to call attention to a growing protest within contemporary theology itself against this eclipse and the traditional historical-critical methods of interpretation that have brought it about. Against the background of the eclipse of emphasis on biblical narrative and literal sense and against the background of the contemporary debate concerning these matters, the difference between modern critical hermeneutics and the hermeneutics required by the nature of the biblical text may be clarified.

The disciplines of biblical studies and biblical theology are passing from one stage into another. In 20 years titles of books and articles such as the following have accumulated in large numbers: "Cosmology, Ontology, and the Travail of Biblical Language," by Langdon Gilkey[1]; "The Superiority of Pre-critical Exegesis," by David Steinmetz[2]; *Biblical Theology in Crisis*, by Brevard Childs[3]; and *The End of the Historical-Critical Method* by Gerhard Maier.[4] As received views are coming increasingly under critical scrutiny in all of the sciences, in part due to the explorations in the foundations of scientific knowledge of such notable figures as Karl Popper and Thomas Kuhn, so too biblical studies and biblical theology have not been able to escape the storm. Biblical scholars once spoke confidently of the "higher critical method"; but today the common sentiment on the growing edge of theological literature is critical of the higher critical method itself. "Never," comments Yale Professor of Old Testament, Brevard Childs, "has the disagreement been greater even regarding the most elementary points of (the Bible's) message. Never has the Bible been the object of more scholarly speculation than today." Historical critics, Childs continues, claimed that their approach

> would sweep away once and for all 'the barrenness of dogmatics.' And yet how many of our seminary-trained

> pastors conscientiously work through the *International Critical Commentary*, or for that matter the more recent *Interpreter's Bible*, and come away with the sense of frustration and utter sterility. There is little which quickens the mind, and nothing which touches the heart.[5]

If one were to cite any one problem that captures best the central issue at stake in the debate between defenders of the traditional critical status quo in biblical studies on the one hand and its new critics on the other it would be the idea that Scripture has one meaning and that to establish it the scholar must be left alone in the company of the author. Higher critical scholarship has been borne along on the premise that the Bible's literal sense reduces itself, when all is said and done, to the original meaning of the text, to the intention of the *human* author. Moreover, it is thought that really to get at this primitive meaning behind the text, which is the meaning against which all others must be checked, historical-critical method and *Sitz im Leben* analysis are the best tools we have.

It is against this view that a chorus of voices—from Paul Ricoeur and Hans-Georg Gadamer in philosophical hermeneutics to Brevard Childs, Hans Frei, and Charles Wood in biblical studies and systematic theology—is being raised in protest. "What is indeed to be understood . . . in a text?" asks Paul Ricoeur. Sounding a sentiment shared by many in the hermeneutical discussion, Ricoeur responds with special straightforwardness:

> Not the intention of the author, which is supposed to be hidden behind the text; not the historical situation common to the author and his original readers; not the expectations or feelings of these original readers; not even their understanding of themselves as historical and cultural phenomena. What has to be appropriated is the meaning of the text itself, conceived in a dynamic way as the direction of thought opened up by the text.[6]

In the context of the interpretation of Scripture this conception of understanding is equivalent to the search for the literal sense of what the text says, the discernment of which, Brevard Childs has concluded, "lies at the heart of one of the most difficult and profound theological questions in the entire study of the Bible."[7]

Arguing that the conflation of the literal sense with the original meaning is fatal to the study of the Bible, Charles Wood has sought to call attention to another concept of the literal sense. For pre-critical exegesis, Wood and many others have contended, the literal sense is the meaning intended by God, which is comprehensible to the reader who participates in the community of faith and which requires no critical operations on the text to determine.[8] The realization of the text as God's Word to us and not just as a historical source of religious traditions happens in the Christian community of faith, within a Christian framework of understanding. In this community and inherited framework, the reader is initiated into the skills and tools to read Scripture according to its overall canonical meaning.

Without this framework of Christian understanding, Wood argues, the obvious sense becomes opaque. A major thesis of Wood's book is thus that philosophical and critical hermeneutics have become the framework of understanding of the Bible and that therefore the notion of literal sense has itself fallen into disrepute. Shifting attention to the engendering experience outside the text, modern historical criticism has lost interest in the literal sense as understood by pre-critical exegesis, and thus also of the role of the community of faith in the interpretation of Scripture.

It must be stressed, moreover, that as this shift took place, interpretation became the business of experts, as Wood argues:

> The literal sense is plainly evident only to a reader who has sufficient mastery of the *usus loquendi* in which the text has its life to read it without undue perplexity. If the *usus* to be heeded is that of the writer or first readers of a biblical text, then naturally we who do not share it are obliged to yield to those who, by virtue of their scholarly expertise can manage to enter into it . . . . Yet, however valuable such an

understanding may be to the church, there is a *usus* of Scripture which has a prior claim to the church's attention, namely the *usus* which establishes its canonical sense as God's self-disclosive Word. It is this canonical sense of the text which the church has most reason to acknowledge as the literal sense of scripture . . . .[9]

With the help of the convincing reflections of Erich Auerbach and Hans Frei on the nature of biblical narrative and its eclipse,[10] we shall at this point take a closer look at how "literal sense" became separated from what the text itself says and depicts. Moreover, we shall also see how the sense of what texts say becomes grounded in and oriented to a reference *behind* the text on whose basis the explicative sense of the text is thought alone able to be established. As this movement occurs the Bible's ability to be interpreted on its own urgings (*sui ipsius interpres*) becomes increasingly subverted. The changed Enlightenment framework in which the Bible becomes approached (the *non-canonical* reconstruction of historical events) comes now to determine the Bible rather than the Bible the framework out of which its reader interprets.

Both Auerbach and Frei contrast the so-called precritical reading of Scripture as literal, straightforward, realistic, and history-like narration to modern, post-Enlightenment approaches. I shall follow essentially Auerbach for a statement of what is meant by literal sense, narrative depiction, and the *realistic* representation of reality in the Bible. Auerbach's analysis will be utilized up to that point in the western representation of reality in literature where the realistic reading begins to break down. At this point we will pick up and present the work of Frei, whose major accomplishment has been to show through what steps the narrative form of the biblical text became bypassed in the post-Reformation period.

## The Realistic Representation
## of Reality in the Bible

Auerbach describes the biblical text as "realistic narrative." By "realistic" is meant that the biblical language is straightforward, direct, simple, and non-contrived. It is the language of ordinary events and common sense that takes the world as we experience it for granted. Depiction hence becomes the way of describing what happens and true historical reference becomes the natural concomitant of making literal sense. Summing up Auerbach's view, Frei says, "The words and sentences meant what they said, and because they did so they accurately described real events and real truths that were rightly put only in those terms and no others."[11]

Typology and figuration are, moreover, according to Auerbach, a logical extension of the plain sense of what is said. Figuration is the extension of the literal sense to the whole text so that it renders a single world.[12] Typology and figuration connect narratives to one another to form a single whole or con-figuration. Naturally this is possible only on the assumption of the providential design of God—the assumption that every character appearing in the narrative sustains a vertical relation to God and that this relation is analogous to the relation that other characters in the narrative sustain to the transcendent.

The events and persons appearing in the biblical record do not represent earthly realities with heavenly meanings (allegory). Heaven only knows what the limits of interpretation could be if this were the case. Rather, events and persons in the narrative typify other events and persons in the same narrative, in the same ongoing drama that has a single overarching meaning in the divine plan. The narrative itself provides its own means, conditions and limits of interpretation.

Figuration is thus closely linked to repetition. The same situations and figures return repeatedly. New persons and events are depicted in relation to old ones in the Bible and by the addition of each new event or person so described, a repetition occurs that contains progress. Finally a cumulative story is created that presses on to a higher, eschatological plane.

Having said this about the "realistic narrative" of Scripture, Auerbach draws the following hermeneutical consequences. Because the religious (providence and the relationship to God) is made concrete in the sensible matter of everyday life in the Bible, that is, because the depiction is realistic and history-like, Auerbach argues that "The Bible's claim to truth . . . is tyrannical, . . . (excluding) all other claims." The Bible insists that its world, in which God and man, heaven and earth, are in dynamic relation to one another in all of the events of ordinary life and history, is the true account of the real world. Thus Auerbach can say that for the Bible "All other scenes, issues, and ordinances have no right to appear independently of it, and it is promised that all of them, the history of all mankind, will be given their due place within its frame, will be subordinated to it." Concludes Auerbach, "The Scripture stories do not . . . court our favor, they do not flatter us that they may please us and enchant us—they seek to subject us and if we refuse to be subjects we are rebels."[13]

Drawing out the consequences for our understanding of the course of life's events, Auerbach claims the Old Testament presents not a *Heilsgeschichte* nor a meditation on special, supranatural experiences, but a "universal history," beginning with creation and ending with the Last Days. Thus "Everything else that happens in the world can only be conceived as an element in this sequence; into it everything that is known about the world . . . must be fitted as an ingredient of the divine plan . . . ." Whatever renders everyday life and ordinary history must be understood in the light of the biblical world-historical frame. That the biblical depiction involves the sublime does not lead away from reality but directly to it.

Moving from realistic narrative depiction in Scripture to later reenactments, Auerbach focuses special attention on the medieval religious drama and its continuation of the reading of Scripture as realistic narrative. In the drama as it develops through the medieval period, Auerbach takes note of the fact that increasingly the reenactment becomes filled out with contemporary life. This is what one might expect from a community and culture in which the biblical claim to shape and direct the world of the observer and believer is taken seriously.

At a crucial point, however, according to Auerbach, a shift takes place, a shift from the incorporation into the narrative of the secular course of events to "secularization." Secularization, Auerbach argues, occurs when "the secular action becomes independent; that is, when human actions outside of Christian world history, as determined by Fall, Passion, and Last Judgment, are represented in a serious vein; when in addition to this manner of conceiving and representing human events, with its claim to be the true and only valid one, other ways of doing so become possible."[14] Below we shall look more closely at this problem of the so-called "independence of the secular action," that is, we shall have to ask about the implications of this for hermeneutics and for our thesis about the relationship of explication to authorial intention and meaning as significance.

## The Eclipse of Biblical Narrative

It is the accomplishment of Hans Frei to have shown how the realistic narrative form of the biblical text became eclipsed in the post-Reformation period. Whereas in the realistic representation of reality it was thought that the text as a whole, and thus as received, offers its own framework of interpretation, Frei shows how Deists and the Rational Religionists established the explicative meaning of texts by reference to extra-textual points of orientation. There occurred then a separation between what the text says and what the text means, as if the two were not concomitant. For Frei the first step in the loss of interest in narrative rendering and the realistic representation of reality involves centrally the matter of reference, of meaning coming to be viewed as having to do with reference.

Frei's argument is that reference became viewed in two possible ways, both having the same debilitating net effect. First, there was the separation of the text's explicative sense—the clarification and explanation of what is said—from its supposed meaning, with meaning involving primarily the text's so-called "ostensive" reference. The prime example of an 18th century thinker in which this first occurred, according to Frei, is Anthony Collins. In Collins the plain sense of what the text says became identified with a text's description of and reference to "a state of affairs known or assumed on independent probable grounds to agree or disagree with the stated proposition."[15] The meaning of a text (one had, of course, immediately to think in atomistic terms) is the extra-textual "spatiotemporal occurrence . . . to which it refers." Allow me a rather lengthy quotation from Frei summarizing the significance of Collins' innovation:

> First, by taking account of the human author's intention as an independent factor, no matter whether his statement finally turns out to make sense in agreement or disagreement with that intention, Collins introduced a new element into the hermeneutical situation of biblical study. He was not alone; it was a typical move in that era in adducing the principles of textual interpretation, quite different from previous affirmation of the unity of intention with linguistic use. It is an important step in preparing the way for the practitioners of historical-critical method. Why scan the heavens speculatively when from the written word, from knowledge of historical conditions and the way human beings think, one can ascertain with great probability what the immediate and human rather than remote divine author has in mind? A few generations later, historical critics were to go on from there and suggest that while the author is indeed important, his intention is but one clue to the meaning of his words. The influence of an author's culture over his mind and outlook came to play a larger role than his conscious intention in the historian's determination of the meaning of his words. The words

become a clue, though not necessarily the only one, to the mind of the author where, rather than in the words alone, meaning resides. To this situation it makes little difference that in some philosophical views the mind is passive and sensation controlled while in others it is not. *The location of meaning outside the statement and inside the author's intention is complemented by a similar condition at the other end of the reach of the notion of meaning.* There it is located, once again, not merely in the words but in the external reality to which the words refer. When this view is applied to the interpretation of scripture the implication is obvious. At both ends of the spectrum the use of language is governed by a sense of the setting for meaningfulness quite different from what had hitherto been prevalent in exegetical practice and accompanying theory. *The immediacy of the world depicted and rendered accessible by the biblical words, and the rich but orderly and interconnected variety of levels of meaning they presented, faded away.* Instead the connection between language and its context is the reality of the author on the one hand and of the single, external reference of the words on the other.[16]

We are all relatively familiar with the theological controversy that this separation between the non-referential narrative sense of what utterances of a text say on the one hand and ostensive historical reference on the other precipitated. The terms of the controversy were accepted by all: namely that the crucial matter determining the meaning of any particular narrative text had to do with its reference to external states of affairs, whether historical personages or events. "The historical referent—the factual history which claims to be revelation—governs and is the test for the explicative sense of the texts. They make sense to the extent that they can be shown to refer, and refer faithfully, to these events."[17] Within this framework of agreement in which literal sense became separated from historical or ostensive reference, heated intramural differences of opinion could emerge with respect to the reliability of the putative facts recorded in biblical narrative. The conservative camp became preoccupied to defend the biblical record as historically reliable, that when

referring to personages as actually having lived, or occur-
rences as actually having taken place, these documents
could be considered trustworthy. Rationalists and critics
on the other hand doubted and denied the historical
reliability of the narratives, especially if and when
reference was ostensively being made to miraculous occur-
rences or the fulfillment of prophecy.

The second form of reference abetting the Enlightenment eclipse of biblical narrative Frei calls "ideal
reference." Apparently there was more than one way to
get rid of what the narrative says. Ideal reference became a
prominent avenue to establish the explicative meaning of
biblical narrative once the unity of historical reference and
religious significance came apart. Especially among the so-
called critical who cast suspicion over, or even rejected, the
historical reliability of biblical narrative, the question of
the remaining possible religious significance of the Bible
became urgent. Even if the narrative is unreliable, the
question arises whether it can nonetheless have a true
theological or moral sense. And, as Frei shows, in fact
most historical critics—Reimarus is a notable excep-
tion—continued to maintain that biblical teaching involves
valuable moral truth. In other words, most felt that the
religious significance of basic biblical beliefs could be
defended as meaningful. Frei calls thinkers who adopt this
position "soft apologists."

In any case, to defend the meaningfulness of even
biblical narratives that relate unfavorably and unreliably
to historical fact, an ideal framework of meaning that "all
right-thinking men can or should be able to recognize"[18]
had to be assumed, a framework which could be established on independent rational grounds. There had thus to
be pre-given an ideal, antecedent, and concomitant context
within which the narrative could be interpreted and de-
coded.

For example, the Genesis story of creation and fall could
thus become viewed as a specifically Jewish *illustration* of
the ubiquity of disruption and lost innocence, or of the
person's present sense of tension between what is and what

ought to be. For those who used such "ideal" references or correlations to determine the meaning of a given narrative, the specific story of creation and fall could no longer be the specific history of Adam in terms of which contemporary experience has to be understood, to which contemporary experience has to be connected as antitype, and into which our personal histories have thus to be incorporated. From the vantage point of biblical narrative, even its reader's sinfully disrupted existence must be viewed concretely as a part of this specific history of creation and fall.

According to Frei, in addition to the idea that meaning is ostensive reference, the specific effort of correlating biblical narrative with an ideal conception also "succeeded in reversing the direction of the interpretation of the biblical stories from pre-critical days, so that they now made sense by their inclusion in a wider frame of meaning."[19] Neither historical critic nor soft apologist was able to take seriously the narrative shape and urging of the biblical stories. Whether in the case of historical critics, their conservative antagonists, or the soft apologist, there emerged a shared eclipse of biblical narrative, of non-referential explication. The watershed difference between the imagination underlying this new situation on the one hand and the older pre-critical scheme in which the literal sense was at once also historical is the fulcrum of Frei's argument.

According to Frei, for the older Protestants, as already for Augustine, the Bible is "a coherent world of discourse in its own right, whose depictions and teachings had a reality of their own, though to be sure, it was the reality into which all men had to fit, and in one way or another did fit."[20] Not only were earlier depictions in the biblical narrative thought analogous to later ones on the assumption of a providentially governed history, but "every present moral and historical experience had been fitted into it"[21] as well. For post-Enlightenment Christianity, however, "It is no exaggeration to say that all across the theological spectrum the great reversal had taken place: interpretation was a matter of fitting the biblical story into another world

with another story rather than incorporating that world into the biblical story."[22] Both the historical and the ideal
way of knowing had in fact become independent ways
laden with foreign narrative elements not so easily recon-
ciliable with the biblical framework.

## Literal Sense and
## the Special Character of
## Theological Hermeneutics

In the realistic representation of reality in narrative, the
literal sense of Scripture as canon of the Christian community has priority. For this reason Christian theology is
concerned especially with the rules and principles whereby
the meaning of what is said in texts gets established. Interpretation is not sharply distinguished from *explication de
text*. Moreover, because theology deals with the biblical
text, regarded as authoritative, it must develop a concept
of hermeneutics commensurate with its special circumstances. In fact, because of these special circumstances, Christian theology is bound to offer a model
of biblical interpretation that is not only not necessarily
germane to other disciplines, but also one that has a rather
*ad hoc* character.[23] By *ad hoc* is meant that theological
method must be relative and flexible, being subservient to
the content that the text itself supplies. The mind of
the text must form not only the content of the text as interpreted by its reader but the very methods by which the text
is investigated. Since the text of Scripture makes a claim on
all, even by regarding those that ignore it as rebels, the
theoretical and critical separation between text and reader
that modern hermeneutics takes for granted on the
assumption of the autonomy of the human subjectivity is
inappropriate to biblical interpretation at the fundamental
level.

The conception of hermeneutics which has been
developed in modern philosophy and on the basis of work

with texts that are judged to be ordinary and nonauthoritative represents a conception that differs then in important respects from theological hermeneutics. This modern conception focuses on the *subject* of knowledge and thus includes the concession that interpretations of these texts tell us as much about the interpreter as about the interpreted. Hermeneutics so conceived focuses on the *external* relations that texts sustain to their various contexts, orginating or contemporary. In this version of hermeneutics attention then shifts from the text to the *context*, i.e. literally to what *accompanies* the text. In short hermeneutics becomes conceivable as a discipline or philosophy concerned with understanding in general. One of its great spokespersons was Friedrich Schleiermacher and its account of that process of understanding would go somewhat as follows.

In the process of the interpretation of texts, the reader normally reads in terms of his own conception of things. Equipped with assumptions and predispositions, the reader reads in terms of a vision (*Weltanschauung*) by which he thinks and to which he is committed. Whether consciously or spontaneously, he thinks, reads and interprets in his own terms, even in dealing with texts that contain assumptions, dispositions, and visions that are not his own. The reader's set of subjective givens comes upon the givens of the text and the subjective givens of its author. It is in the interplay of those two that understanding is defined.

Let us call the set of terms relative to which the reader reads, the reader's "subtext." As the reader enters the world of the text before him, he confronts terms, images, and thoughts that are partially familiar, but also partially unfamiliar. The unfamiliar becomes illuminated by the familiar in the text and the familiar in the text is what is similar to the reader's own subtext, the reader's own world of terms, images, and presuppositions. It is through the medium of the familiar in both reader and text then that the reader decodes what he reads as he attempts to understand the author who stands behind the text and gave rise to it.[24]

It is one of the major claims of this present discussion

that such a hermeneutic, though not necessarily mistaken generally, is inappropriate to biblical interpretation at the most fundamental religious level, where a common sense approach should dictate the way of understanding. Modern critical hermeneutics often works with the distinctions between text and reader and between text and author as separations. Often these separations represent attempts to ground (and thus dissolve) the text and what it says the way it says it in the interpreter's non-textual reconstruction of events. The *context* of the text becomes dominant and "the context" proves most often to be *the interpreter's own speculative conception* of that context and thus not simply the context itself. Through these steps interpretation becomes removed from the text and what it says, ending up in the interpreter's suppositions and speculations, or in the author's putative subjectivity and historical situation.

Critical approaches to Scripture more often than not in their way invalidate the narrative claim and power of the biblical text. If one begins with secularized concepts of meaning and reference, interpretation and fact, Scripture gets taken out of its own Christian framework of understanding. In 18th and 19th century Liberal theology, this is what has happened, so that the character of the biblical text has lost its force and become undermined in hermeneutics.

Where secularistic theory is granted an approved place, it is no wonder that there would emerge a conflict between scientific scholarship and biblical faith. However, in the "best" historical-critical literature this conflict is not only acknowledged but regarded as a bonus as well. Working with a Lutheran view of justification by faith, such noted critics as Bultmann, Käsemann, and Ebeling emphasize its epistemological implications. According to these theologians, scientific theories have demolished any hope to found or rest faith on a noetic or intellectual base. Moreover, exactly this is judged to be their benefit to faith. As Bultmann expresses it in his famous 1952 essay on demythologization:

Radical demythologization is the parallel to the Pauline-Lutheran doctrine of justification apart from works of the law by faith alone. Or rather, it is its consistent application in the sphere of knowledge. Just as the doctrine of justification, it destroys all man's false security and all false longing for security, whether that security rests on his good behavior or on his validating knowledge. The man who will believe in God as his God must know he has nothing in his hand in which he might believe, that he is, as it were, up in the air, and can demand no proof for the truth of the word addressing him. For the ground and object of faith are identical. Only he finds security who lets all security go, who—to speak with Luther—is prepared to go into the inner darkness.[25]

Rendering everything doubtful, historical criticism leaves faith to depend on itself and thus on God alone.

For those less dialectically inclined in their view of faith and reason, historical criticism, when taken to the final stage of its consequences, has led to a surrender of Christianity, as the famous Tübingen church historian and form critic, Franz Overbeck, claimed and as his biography illustrates. From the moment Protestant theology borrowed the methods of historical criticism from the secular sciences, according to Overbeck, theology was doomed to become the grave digger of Christianity. Those who make use of modern scientific methods, Overbeck argues, must recognize that it is "part and parcel of the secularization of Christianity, a luxury which it allows itself but which, like all luxuries, can be had only for a price."[26]

In a recent, important work, Joachim Kahl, a biblical scholar turned atheist, concludes the same.[27] Insistent on the fact that the New Testament gives us a clear picture only of what the early Christian community believed about Jesus, historical criticism, according to Kahl, separates the beliefs of that community from the realities to which they were intended to refer. These latter realities are thought essentially inaccessible to thought. According to Kahl, a life-long student of the works of Bultmann, Käsemann, and Ebeling, the record of historical criticism has demonstrated "the impossibility of ever getting a glimpse of the historical Jesus,"[28] since the latter is "totally buried under the rubbish of primitive Christian myths and legends."[29] Accordingly Kahl charges that the residue of Christian commitment present in the theologies of Ebeling, Bultmann, and Käsemann, who ostensibly exercise criticism radically, represents an arbitrary escape into "the world of pious aspirations."[30] Especially the Bultmannian program of demythologization is called a "romantic attempt to vindicate the honour of the Christian faith," and "a modern way of playing the same game theologians have been playing professionally for a very long time indeed— the manipulation of authoritative texts so that they can still be put to use today . . . ."[31] Bultmann's existentialistic interpretation of texts and failure to take seriously what the authors of the Bible say the way they say it is dubbed as cynicism born of an apologetical necessity.[32]

From this situation we must conclude that a specifically theological hermeneutic seems appropriate to the biblical text at the fundamental level. The only other option seems to be a new, general hermeneutical theory that takes genuinely seriously the reality of transcendent revelation and its communication to man in scriptural form. The modern, historically and critically oriented form of interpretation may be "acceptable" outside of the Christian framework of understanding and thus outside of the context of believing affirmation of the text of Scripture as authoritative and normative. But such interpretation seems inappropriate within the Christian religious community, where the Bible is most at home, because such interpretation is prevented from bringing about radical subjection and belief. When applied to Scripture, the critical form of interpretation undermines the text's claim and thus vitiates its true character. The Bible must be allowed to dictate its own rules, rules that get at the text through what it says the way it says it and rules thus that give priority to the literal and typological sense of Scripture as shared by the Christian community of faith. The only genuine Christian framework for interpreting the Bible is the canonical one.

Having called our attention to this is the significance of the work of Auerbach and Frei.

## Chapter V

# The Phenomenon of Ordinary Use and the Creation-Fall-Redemption-Consummation Structure of Biblical Narrative

*"In the naive posture of thought, which the believing community occupies as it appropriates the narrative as presented, we naively derive the creation-fall-redemption-consummation scheme in continued exposure to the text as we now have it . . . .*

*"In the direct and full reading of Scripture that occurs in the community of faith, a pattern for which has been established in the traditions of Christian orthodoxy, the story of the Bible is the story of God's creation of a perfect world, man's subsequent rebellion and fall from spiritual perfection, the Lord's plan—centering in Jesus Christ—of the restoration of his lost creation and people, and God's completion of all things . . . in eternal life."*

# The Phenomenon of Ordinary Use and the Creation-Fall-Redemption-Consummation Structure of Biblical Narrative

In our discussion of Scripture and Spirit and in our elaborations on the idea of a direct and ordinary use of the Bible, we have dealt with the question of how, formally speaking, Scripture exercises its authority. Though criticism is not fond of the story of the Bible as phenomenally there in the text of the whole as we now have it, in naive reading the story or narrative of Christianity is readily transmitted to people in pre-deconstructed form. We have emphasized this primary level of Bible-use in the community of faith. Moreover, we have done this on the assumption that the text of Scripture is the locus of its authority and that the Bible's message is communicated to its readership in a full and relatively common sensical manner. What becomes thus transmitted in the community of faith over years of sifting and careful exposure to the narrative of the Bible is the given content of the Bible (what one might also call the structure of Christian orthodoxy).

Moreover, this given content is the subject-matter with which scientific study of the Bible must subsequently come to terms. Sound scientific study of the Bible does not deconstruct the structure of the Christian narrative as apprehended in the situation of givenness. We shall speak later (Chapter VI) about how Christian scientific theology (our alternative to criticism) should work with the subject-matter of the Bible as manifested in the phenomenon of reverent reading, Christian sermonizing, and ordinary use. Here it will be our purpose to venture a concrete, content-specific statement about *what* it is that is yielded in the phenomenon of the Bible's regular and ordinary use. What is the Christian story or narrative? What is the story that is objectively presented there and relative to which the believing community subsequently interprets other texts and even life experience itself?

When speaking of the structure of biblical narrative, I mean to be talking about the normative in the Christian's text. By "normative" is not meant the provincial, the particular, and wholly contingent in what the Christian derives from Scripture in reading it for what it says. Nor do I mean to refer to this or that idea, teaching, or doctrine (such as justification by faith), which is invariably only a part of the whole.[1] Our inquiry seeks to make reference to the structure of the Christian narrative, to what in the 19th century was called, somewhat unfortunately, the "essence" of Christianity. What we have in mind is that salient web of themes[2] that lend to the Christian's text its unity and distinctiveness. Some theologians have spoken helpfully in this connection of Christianity's "fundamental motif" because the Christian's master code is a text, a narrative, a story, and not a vast catena of authoritative truths that were all created equal.[3]

The latter view of the Christian's text is deficient on many counts. For one, it does not comport with the given form and shape of Scripture. Scripture as a whole is neither a legal code nor a tractatus of logia. In these latter forms of text there predominates an evenness of materials that is absent from Scripture as a whole. While some sub-blocks of Scripture like the Decalogue or Proverbs might seem to have a form similar to a legal code or collections of logia, Scripture as a whole, as canon, does not.

As canon Scripture bears greatest similarity to the narrative texts of literature.[4] In Scripture there is a storyline, a range of scenes and acts through which, as ordered in a sequence, a thread has been woven. There is a motion from beginning to end. Moreover, there is in the overall story falling and rising action and the interaction of characters and circumstances through which identities are revealed.[5] There is in short an unfolding drama about God's relationship to the world.

It is crucial to notice this dramatic character of scriptural narrative.[6] For the form of Scripture communicates to its readers something of the essence of its content and of its perspective on human life itself. According to Scripture, there is in all things a tendency, a trend, a direction, and a dramatic core.[7] When we fail to notice the character of Scripture as dramatic narrative, we reduce the text of Scripture to the abstractions of the mind. We tap the conflict out of the text and subsequently out of our view of human life as well, to the extent that we let the text determine our world view. Rationalism and the narrative form of Scripture are incompatible.

As we attempt to describe the scriptural fundamental motif, we shall thus not be presenting a systematic theology in brief outline. We shall of course be talking about that in the Bible which makes non-narrative discourse and subsequent systematization possible. In addition we shall be depending on classic reflections of the faith that are efforts to get at what the text of the Bible as a whole says. Finally, we shall not be offering a survey of the various atomistic results of biblical studies, as if the so-called "facts" might subsequently secret a comprehensive view of the whole. Our way through the Christian's scriptural text must be another way, the way of the story, the structure of the narrative as a whole.

The fundamental motif of Scripture is creation-fall-redemption-consummation.[8] This is the order or sequence of the narratives and events recorded *as they address us*. This is the pattern according to which God has executed his purpose, at least for all we can know, since the Bible is the only information we have. Thus this is the pattern as viewed from the high ground that God himself occupies. The Bible is the revelation of God's Word, which he has himself authored. The Bible gives its recipients a privileged look at things. The Bible's recipients are most prone to view the whole story from the lapsarian place that they occupy in it or from the place that its human authors occupied. But the Bible is addressed to us from God and by God and is about what he has done in the way and sequence in which he has done it.

The Bible's perspective and layout are, we might say, theocentric, not objectifying and mythological, as critical literature often claims. Such a latter view of what the text's vantage point and content really are is only sure of (and thus begins with) the *human* ground on which the text rests. The text of the Bible, rationalistically deconstructed in terms of that human base, naturally places redemption first, even sometimes building a lapsarian element into creation itself. Rather than claim that the Bible objectifies, we would say that critical reconstructions subjectivize and anthropocentrize the text of the Bible. Beginning as they do with the order in which man (or the community) comes to know and present its knowledge of God, other views of the Bible's pattern than the theocentric focus on the historical, cultural, social, and psychological origins of the text. These view the Bible as essentially a product of human culture.

Moreover, in the naive posture of thought, which the believing community occupies as it appropriates the narrative as presented, we naively derive the creation-fall-redemption-consummation scheme in continued exposure to the text as we now have it. The church does not deconstruct and then speculatively, anthrocentristically reconstruct the story before it is ready to accept it. The church rather lives by the story and sees to it that that story gets passed on to its successive generations. The scheme of the Bible's story as described above (creation first, redemption later) is thus the flow of events reflected in every child's story Bible, in the church's ritual, in its simplest and most comprehensive confessions (for example, in the Apostles' Creed), and in the order of its liturgical year. It is the scheme of things that has been passed on throughout the history of the church because the church repeats the major typical stories and makes sense of them in the theocentric order in which they are given in the text itself. What is crucial is the content and depiction of the biblical text, not the cultural and historical context out of which its human writers composed its various parts.

In the direct and full reading of Scripture that occurs in the community of faith, a pattern for which has been established in the traditions of Christian orthodoxy, the story of the Bible is the story of God's creation of a perfect world, man's subsequent rebellion and fall from spiritual perfection, the Lord's plan—centering in Jesus Christ—of the restoration and restitution of his lost creation and people, and God's completion of all things in the end and fulfillment of them in eternal life. This is the storyline powerfully and unmistakably suggested by the placement first in the Bible of the story of Adam and Eve and the placement of the Gospels later. This placement suggests strongly that the story of Jesus must be interpreted and seen on the backdrop of the story of Adam and Eve's creation and fall. Moreover, this sequence and order is reinforced by the placement of the Old Testament first in the canon, an interpretative decision made in the canonization process that has more significance than modern theology is inclined to grant.

In modern theology, as in much modern science, an odd reversal of the proper relationship of life and science has taken place. Appearance and reality were distinguished; moreover appearance was equated with the account of it offered in traditional, pre-modern, Aristotelian philosophy, which was in turn dubbed *naive* and *realistic* by post-Cartesians and Lochean empiricists.[9] What is real came in turn to be identified with a reconstructed image of the world order, an image based on what the new methods of the then emerging natural sciences were able to handle.

Hence, the appearance of diverse things and qualities in naive experience was reduced in science to the unity and universality of an underlying, usually mathematical or natural scientific, substantial reality.[10]

Among modern theologians most acknowledge the pattern of orthodoxy as corresponding to the structure of biblical narrative. At the same time, however, most of these theologians would regard that unmistakable pattern and the corresponding shape of the canon as more apparent than real. The phenomenally given pattern masks—because it is objectified—a deeper, real structure that only analysis can uncover. For modern theology it would be naive, in the bad sense of the word, to regard the apparent as essential and meaningful. Though to the naive realist the structure of biblical narrative is creation-fall-redemption-consummation, a scientifically reconstructed view of the text of the Bible reveals that another narrative lies at the heart of the Christian story. Some say it is the pattern of election-reconciliation,[11] others the scheme of return to God through the evolution of the cosmic process toward the Christic form.[12] But most agree that the creation-fall-redemption-consummation sequence is phenomenally there in the Bible, that it does represent the pre-scientific world view of the Bible's human authors and redactors, but that it would thus be pre-critical to adopt it today.[13]

In addition to the pattern that emerges in the direct use of the Bible in the community of faith, there are these patterns as established again and again through the decades and centuries and finally codified in the form of credal responses of the Christian community to Scripture. The early creeds recapitulate Scripture's storyline. The Apostolic Creed (third century A.D.) preserves and reproduces the Scripture's own order and structure of presentation of the acts of God, even though we only become aware and conscious of God's works through Jesus Christ. In fact the scriptural order and structure was repeated in the Creed against considerable pressure to place the confession concerning Christ (the second article of the Creed) up front and first. That primitive confession (no creed but Christ) was after all the prominent or even exclusive one in the New Testament community, as Oscar Cullmann has shown.[14] Since the new community had separated itself specifically from the Jewish synagogue and then specifically only on the question of who Jesus was, the belief in God the Father Almighty, Maker of heaven and earth remained strictly implicit and undisputed in the new community. Naturally that belief in the Father God was there all along insofar as the Scripture of the Old Testament was taken for granted. Only later, in the second and third century conflict with the Gnostics, who denied that the good God who saves us in Christ is the same as the God who created the world, did the confession concerning God, the Father emerge expressly.[15] But even though this article emerged expressly later than the confession concerning Christ, the implicit, naive order prevailed in the composition and arrangement of the articles of the Apostolic Creed, and thus the confession concerning the Father's work in creation was placed first. This naive order of the biblical storyline continued in the post-New Testament era to determine the consciousness of the Christian community.

In our discussion of how direct, reverent reading and what it yields is related to the scientific study of the Bible, we shall see how much modern theology has come to challenge this scheme as legendary, mythological, and naive in the negative sense of the term. We shall also try to present some reasons for theology's inability to accept this phenomenal pattern of giveness as determinative for the interpretation of other things in the Bible. At this point, however, an explication of the structural pattern that orders the Bible is necessary. What is the meaning—content-wise—of this fundamental theme that is yielded in reading the Bible in the pre-scientific setting of the Christian community's faith and praxis?

First, the scriptural narrative includes images that convey the cosmic proportions (existence) within which the ongoing story is placed. There is the "something" to which the lapsarian and redemptive modifications happen. In the Bible this is called "creation." The scriptural story is a story of origins, of the connection between transcendence and immanence, of the spiritual quality and status of the world and man, and of the nature and structure of the cosmic arena within which the ongoing drama of divine-human interaction takes place.

The narrative of the Bible is unmistakably a story of the cosmos. It has become popular since Hegel's time to pit the so-called *historical* perspective of Israelite religion over against the so-called *cosmologizing* tendency of ancient Greece. However, the story of the Bible is, on the face of it, necessarily cosmological. It presents a view of the framework within which human destiny will take place. Moreover, it presents a view of the structures of order and discipline within which, according to the Bible, life will develop and in keeping with which it will be sustained. The world of the Bible is not just a world of persons, divine-human encounters, and the revelation of the divine identity. It is also a story about the creation of the world and what it was that *resulted* from that divine activity. An action theory of the world will not do.[16]

Moreover, in the narrative of the Bible this "element" stands first, being presented both as a radical break in relation to what "was before" and as an introduction to all that is to follow. The story does not begin with God, but rather takes him for granted. "In the beginning, God . . ." says the Bible. The connection between God and the not-god is not continuous, for no theogonic story about God is needed to explain who he is.[17] Furthermore, no story of God's origin is needed to lead into a story about the not-god and what will take place within it. In addition, what gets said about the not-god prepares us properly to understand our present condition and the nature of the remedy to our predicament. The world does not *come out of* God.[18] Rather, it is made by the Word ("And God said, 'Let there be,' and there was"), and is thus wholly contingent. Yet this world and man thus created have a relative life of their own "overagainst" God.[19] As created, man and the world were constituted real and effective substances, with a being of their own separate and distinct from God ("God blessed them and said to them 'Be fruitful and increase in number; fill the earth and subdue it. Rule over the fish of the sea and the birds of the air and over every living creature that moves on the ground' " Genesis 1:28). Created with an essential structure and powers, God's creatures have a given self-activity and are able to function with consequence among themselves.

Moreover, though relative and dependent, the world is very good as made ("And God saw that it was very good.") Though not divine, it is affirmable, the place of man's abode. Within the world as made there is no inbuilt dross.[20] Creation is rather the condition *from which* man falls and accordingly the condition unto which he must be restored. In the Bible there is a persistent resistance to redemption without creation.

Second, there is a story about the disruption that has taken place in the world, between God and man, and between heaven and earth. One of the decisive marks of the biblical narrative is a view and set of images about the fact of fallenness, sin and evil, as well as a storied effort to say wherein the "explanation" of this intrusion lies. Because the story of the fall of man comes *after* his creation in original righteousness, the Bible persists in viewing evil as an intruder. Sin, evil, and their consequences do not belong to the natural or essential order of things. So we are left with the strong impression in the story of Genesis that the disruption that comes is nonoriginal and thus owes nothing to the divine creativity. Sin and evil must necessarily depend on creation; they could not be without it since they are portrayed as modifying it. The imagery of the fall constantly refers back to creation—not as inhering in it but as the perversion of it, and thus as under creation's power.

That evil is a perversion does not mean that evil is not real, that it is not itself a power. Evil is not *privatio boni* but is a dark force to be reckoned with, an active power of resistance to the way in which God oriented the world when he first created it. Its "explanation" moreover as a real power resides, according to the biblical portrayal, within the event of the fall itself and thus within man's agency.[21] Sin and evil are grounded in nothing outside of man's own willful transgression of the divine probation. The power of sin is the power of a perverted *human will* and thus the power of a perverted *human freedom*. It is to be reckoned with because man was originally *created*, i.e., constituted a real and *effective* substance with a being of his own, able to act with consequence among other finite entities. Moreover this original sin of man became all pervasive, misdirecting everything in man and outside of him, and leaving no man unscathed.[22]

It is against this background that the remaining story of the Bible is played out, just as the story of creation is the background against which the story of disruption and fall must be placed. The third part of the scriptural story is the great story of the remedy to the disruption that culminates in the death and resurrection of Christ. Because this story and history is detailed elaborately in the Bible, it is often regarded as the center of the narrative as a whole.[23] Moreover, because the human authors of the Bible all write from the vantage point of the experience of saving responsiveness, the Bible is often called a *Heilsgeschichte*.

It is important to maintain a distinction here. While the whole story of the Bible *originates* out of the situation of faith and forgiveness, the story is itself about more. The Bible's *Heilsgeschichte* is situated in between the great stories of the Beginning and the End and thus requires the two stories that frame it in the sequence in which they appear. Accordingly, the story of the redemption of the world is pre-eminently a story of the coming restoration and restitution of *creation*.

This can be seen in many ways in the Bible. But the most significant is that God consistently is reconciled to the creation and reconciles in terms of it. God's original order sets the terms of the settlement by which man and the world are reconciled to God. This order is thus carefully and painstakingly vindicated. For example, since the created order is a moral and legal order, reconciliation is achieved in legal and forensic terms: Christ the lamb of God is slain as payment for the sins of mankind.[24] Given creation for what it is, redemption could have taken place in no other way than it did. It is then in terms of the conditions of the created order that salvation is achieved and expresses itself as an act of redemption. As the world and man are reconciled to God, they are restored, returned to their original condition of finite integration and at-one-ment with God.

Finally, the work of the Spirit and the consummation represent the effacious application to fallen humanity of the redemption achieved by Christ and the bringing to completion of the restorative process. Biblical images about the range and character of that fulfillment are a strong statement to the effect that the last things repeat the first things. The fires of judgment will annihilate sin, but they will not negate creation. Moreover, creational life will be restored to its norm. Found in Christ, man will become truly man again, not reabsorbed into God's inner life, from out of which, some claim wrongly, he was begotten. There will be no violations of the limits of space and time since they were created very good. According to the general lines of the eschaton as depicted in the Bible,

> Hope awaits the *comprehensive* renewal of creational life and reality. It awaits the comprehensive renewal of *creational* life. More specifically, hope anticipates the redemptive affirmation of creational limits of temporality, relationality, and freedom. These shall be cleansed from sin and its effects and in some senses altered, but they will also be continuous in significant ways with what we now know of these limits.[25]

The one ongoing story of Christianity and the theme of the realistic biblical narrative are made concrete in the images and paradigms of the Bible's story of creation-fall-redemption-consummation. The cumulative story itself in the stages of its unfolding from beginning to end is the fundamental motif of Christianity. The overall structure itself is the essence, not some one thing within or behind it to which the structure must be referred to determine its meaning. Moreover, that structure is yielded directly in reverent reading of the Bible in the community of faith without the performance on the Bible of critical and abstractive operations. The storyline is picked up in the encounter of believing reader and authoritative text. In this situation faith's realities and structures make an impression, create a mind, and are immediately grasped. Moreover, in naive experience repeated practical confirmations and reiterations form faith consciousness and help at various levels (including the theoretical and theological) to separate the spurious from the genuine.

# The Yield of Direct Reading and Its Relationship to Scientific Theology

*"Creation-fall-redemption-consummation as the overall structure of bliblical narrative is the object of reflection in theology. But it should also be the epistemological means (beliefs) by which the researcher's activity of investigation is controlled.*

*"Through the life of faith and obedient, reverent use of the Bible, the Christian community has already achieved certain apprehensions of the meaning of the Word. These utterances about and responses to the self-disclosive Word of God in the Bible should fund the reflective enterprise in a comprehensive sense. Theology and the scholarly study of the Bible should begin with the givenness of these phenomena and respond to them as they appear in the concrete situation of faith."*

## Chapter VI

# The Yield of Direct Reading and Its Relationship to Scientific Theology

Drawing on our earlier distinction between the pre-scientific and the scientific modes of knowledge, we must ask how the two relate, if at all. On the one side of this relation stands the fact of a direct reading and naive rendering of the biblical text in the community of faith. There is the use of the Bible as canon of the Christian church. On the other side of the relation is the scientific study of the Bible as an historical document. This is a second order, reflective inquiry into the Bible which is in character scientific and scholarly and which performs "critical" operations on the text, deliberately bringing to bear upon it knowledge derived from sources other than the Bible.

The crucial question is how, if at all, these two modes are related. Do we have to do here with two separate contexts of meaning that must not be confused? Are there two tracks along each of which we chart an independent course, possibly coming to different results? Are the two ways equivalent and thus essentially unable to be subordinated one to the other? Is it satisfactory to associate piety, meditation, and the believing community's use of the Bible with one track or way and theology and historical study with the other track or way? In other words, is it satisfactory to associate the life of faith with the former and knowledge with the latter?

My own view of this matter presupposes that the life of faith ought not to be hermetically isolated from scientific activity, including the scientific activity of theology and biblical studies. Philosophy distinguishes the object and content of knowledge from the means of knowledge. The object or content of knowledge is the theoretical field a discipline intentionally directs itself to investigate; the means of knowledge is the vantage point, the base of assumptions, from which the investigation is conducted. With that distinction in mind I would wish to argue that for the scientific investigation of the Bible in the disciplines of theology creation-fall-redemption-consummation must be both the subjective perspective with which the researcher operates as well as what he seeks to know. If the Bible's claim and force are not to be undone, the Bible must be investigated by the same mind as it creates in believing affirmation of it. Creation-fall-redemption-consummation as the overall structure of biblical narrative is the object of reflection in theology. But it should also be the epistemological means (beliefs) by which the researcher's activity of investigation is controlled.

As for the object of knowledge, it is already there.[1] It is not the prerogative of theology to interpret the Bible to the church, retailing its specialized information to the unknowing. We do well to reflect on Arnold van Ruler's bold assertion that "theology does not belong in the church."[2] Interpretation of the Bible exists prior to (both logically and temporally) the emergence on the scene of theology as a reflective and abstractive discipline. Through the life of faith and obedient, reverent use of the Bible, the Christian community has already achieved certain apprehensions of the meaning of the Word. These utterances about and responses to the self-disclosive Word of God in the Bible should fund the reflective enterprise in a comprehensive sense. They constitute the pre-scientific epistemological context within which scholarship that is genuinely Christian moves. Theology and the scholarly study of the Bible should begin with the givenness of these phenomena and respond to them as they appear in the concrete situation of faith. Theology should be the interpretation of the interpretation of the Bible that already exists within the community of faith. As K.J. Popma has concluded: "By this road . . . we are led to the idea that the naive use of the Bible is the foundation of all Bible-study, also in its theological elaboration."[3]

Moreover, the Christian framework of understanding originated by the Bible should also be the framework of understanding employed in those disciplines that reflect on the phenomenon of Christian faith. Where this is not so, second order reflection could deprecate, deny, or vitiate what is given and yielded in first-order experience. The integration of faith and learning in the discipline of biblical studies means that the world view investigated in the text must also be accepted as the world view from the vantage point of which the text is investigated. Only under such circumstances is the Bible's total claim properly acknowledged. Where the biblical framework is not taken to be the context for scientific study, the only other option seems to be the acceptance of a fact-value, science-faith distinction in which the two tracks of life in the *ecclesia* and scholarship in the university are scrupulously kept apart.[4] Where scientific theology is not ecclesially funded, it nonetheless continues to be funded pre-theoretically and that usually by the climate of opinion which happens at any given moment to reign within the discipline. Where this latter situation obtains, one finds specifically that the conduct of theological scholarship often takes place on unconscious foundations not so easily reconcilable with the Christian story because in the modern centuries secularism has taken possession of the intellectual field. Unfortunately much modern scientific study of the Bible as an historical source illustrates this all too well.

Whereas scientific study of the Bible could perfect our insight into what's in the Bible, often the biblical world is co-opted by another world view that controls the researcher's method of investigation.[5] Investigations into the foundations (historical and systematic) of biblical criticism have unearthed the world view and paradigm with which post-Enlightenment critical scholarship of Scripture works.[6] Under circumstances in which the Enlightenment framework of understanding is taken for granted, the higher criticism employed in the scientific investigation of Scripture appears as a radical modification of the so-called naive (now understood in the prejorative sense) reading of the Bible as a creation-fall-redemption-consummation story.

In his recent major work *Christian Faith* the Reformed theologian Hendrikus Berkhof argues for the inevitability of this odd reversal.[7] I have shown elsewhere that the fundamental motif of Berkhof's presentation of the Christian faith in this work is the Neo-platonic and Idealistic pattern of "descent from and return to God in a literal, theo-ontological sense." In Berkhof's view "God (motivated by holy love) literally empties himself (in creation) to raise man to share in his being; this requires that God gather up the attributes of his own being as he becomes all in all with his people, who are in process of being elevated to him by means of the evolution of all things to the Christic pattern."[8] I wish to add here that for Berkhof modern higher criticism of the Bible confirms this view. Moreover, according to Berkhof, modern criticism also teaches the non-independence of creation in relation to redemption, and the ideas that all reality is provisional, that there is an inbuilt dross in things, and that, therefore, restorationism is untenable.

According to Berkhof, "historical-critical investigation of the biblical traditions" has made it clear that the confession concerning creation is a *consequence* of the confession concerning salvation.[9] Berkhof thus prefers to link up the historical Jesus Christ and creation, on his view following the express teaching of the New Testament. To this Berkhof contrasts "traditional dogmatics" which viewed the New Testament passages referring to Christ's work in creation as being about the role of the second person of the

Trinity, who as *logos asarkos* later became incarnated in the historical Jesus Christ. Moreover, with this traditional view Berkhof also associates a reading of Genesis 1 and 2 that supports the idea of a "completed world in the 'state of rectitude.' " According to Berkhof's rendition of the traditional view, after a short while "the human race and nature lost this paradisaical state through Adam's fall. Later, however, the second Adam came to restore this state. Salvation thus serves the order of creation," and therefore that order cannot, according to the traditional view, be described in terms of salvation. But according to Berkhof "historical criticism has put an end to this type of thinking."[10]

Why has Prof. Berkhof been driven to this conclusion? My answer to that question may not appear to be direct, but I would contend the following and seek to elaborate on it in the final pages of this essay: Berkhof accepts the modern restriction of knowledge to philosophy, science, and theoretical thought. Hence there can really be no theological *given* for historical criticism of the Bible, no prior normative interpretation of the Bible that it becomes theology's obligation to perfect. Rather, criticism's method of clarifying comes to precede and determine theology's object and content. But because secularism with its implicit narratives about God, man, the world and the relationship of these to one another has come in possession of the scientific field, including theology, scientific study of the Bible that thinks to fund itself more often than not instead finds itself challenging the story of the Bible as apprehended in the situation of givenness with modern narratives deeply inhering in the categories and distinctions with which science works.[11] Because theological method has not been derived from and informed by the object and its first order apprehension in the community of faith, theology finds itself keeping all the Christian narratives but changing their order; or as Langdon Gilkey has argued so convincingly, keeping all the traditional Christian language but changing or equivocating on all the meanings.[12]

The result of this subordination of theological method to secular science has been the gigantic project, in which many a major theologian of every Christian tradition is now enthusiastically engaged, of reinterpreting the biblical world view with its many paradigms and images in the light of modern Enlightenment ones.[13] Where theology does not begin with the phenomenal resources of a pre-theoretical interpretation of the Bible that funds and norms it, theology can no longer be conceived as deepening of insight into and elaboration on the apprehensions of faith given in the mode of a direct use of the Bible in the community of faith. In fact these given apprehensions can become viewed as naive, uncritical, objectivist, and mythological or pre-scientific in the negative sense of these terms. It is just such a view of these apprehensions that inspires the thesis that critical study of the Bible has restricted knowledge that is of any theoretical importance to scientific thought and its results.

I have insisted that the "community's interpretation" of the Bible ought to be the object-matter and means of knowledge of any scientific study of it. For it is in the pre-reflective mode that faith's realities are apprehended. The science of theology is rooted in this theological given where ordinary language and knowledge already register their significance. Because it is incumbent on the science of theology to draw its data from the direct interpretation of Scripture that takes place in the *ecclesia*, we may regard the sense of Scripture thus apprehended as *proto*-scientific. Theology and biblical studies must analyze the processes of meaning-establishment as carried out in the community of faith with its naive grasp of the text and its reiteration of that grasp in its ecumenical summaries, formulas, and creeds. Moreover, theology and biblical studies can make the valuable contribution of completing the picture of the whole as apprehended in faith with vast bodies of detailed information and historical insight. So long as the originary process of interpreting is allowed to show itself and is not occluded as theoretically uninteresting or unimportant, scientific study of the Bible can be a success.

# Conclusion

In conclusion allow me a few remarks about what I am and am not saying by stressing the explicative sense of the text of Scripture as much as I do. First, I do not mean to be denying that determining what the text's literal sense is involves a context of understanding. Throughout I have spoken of a direct and naive reading of the Bible and its importance for scientific theology. On the question of knowing the truth, I share Gadamer's protest against the methodological dogmatism of the scientific era. By siding with Gadamer's phenomenologically oriented concept of the primacy of lived experience and its qualitative difference from theoretical thought, which is derivative and abstractive, I have not meant to leave the impression that pre-scientific life experience is unformed and non-historical! Intellectual tradition, political affiliation, racial background, social-economic status—all of these are generally taken to be distinguishing characteristics of the person that invariably become obstacles in the knowledge of the truth because they prejudice the person and thus give him a skewed grasp of things. In fact, however, it is only through a concrete context of understanding appropriate to the objects being understood that knowledge is possible. The pressing concern then becomes *the appropriate* context of knowledge, not the common attempt in much science to claim absolution from context-determinateness.

Moreover, throughout I have spoken of "reverent" or "believing" reading. By saying "reverent" or "believing," I am of course already placing the text within a certain context, the context of accepting affirmation and identification. From especially Hans Frei and Charles Wood we can learn that the text of Scripture makes sense, literal sense, only within the framework of Christian understanding and faith. If the community and tradition of faith are not presupposed, the literal sense of the text, the text as it has usually been taken, becomes opaque. To paraphrase Wood's argument in particular, we might say that the reason that one man's literal sense is another man's nonsense is that the basic framework (context) of understanding within which the Bible once made literal sense has been altered by the post-Enlightenment world (context) in which we now live.

But, naturally this in turn raises the question of the criterion that determines understanding as *Christian*. It is at this point I believe we can do no better than focus first on the text and say that its explicative sense has logical and epistemological priority over both any other sense and use of the text. The material of the Bible as canonical has priority in an exhaustive sense. Again, it is not that I am denying that the reader comes to the text with certain predispositions. What is contested, however, is that those he comes with may be autonomously established; that other frameworks than the conventional Christian one are appropriate to allow the meaning of the text to be forthcoming.

Second, my stress on the priority of the explicative, literal sense is moreover not intended to pronounce out of order all scientific, theoretical knowledge that might be brought to bear on the text of Scripture to recover its meaning. There might conceivably be disciplines or bodies of scholarship that develop themselves and process data *within* the matrix of a reverent, Christian, canonical understanding of the biblical text. I hold out for the possibility and propriety of scholarship that takes its cue from the explicative meaning of the text and works subsequently to deepen our insight into it. Scholarship then that uses every means possible to serve the illumination of the *Scripture's canonical sense* is wholly appropriate and is what I would call the result of the integration of faith and learning within the discipline of theology itself. What I reject is the view that both the Christian canonical context of understanding and the critical one that undergirds the study of Scripture as a public, historical source are valid in their own right. This latter view limits the range within which Scripture as canon can function and thus sets critical scholarship free to bring to bear upon Scripture itself a secular story about God, man and the world with which Scripture cannot be so easily reconciled. Even the world of theological and historical scholarship must be incorporated in the Christian framework of understanding.

Hence, the point of this essay reduces itself to the notion of the logical or epistemological priority of Scripture over life. Though life (the context within which Scripture originated and toward which it merges) and Scripture correlate, primacy, purity, and exclusive normativity belong to Scripture alone, also within the area of scholarship. Though text and context are inseparable, the text of Scripture must more and more become enlarged so as to incorporate our lives within itself. This means in short that the world within which the Bible finds itself must more and more be made to reflect Scripture, to borrow and draw on its vision and vocabulary. Only in this way can the literal sense again emerge and become the obvious meaning.

# Notes for Chapter I

1. By "direct" I do not intend to exclude what gets known about the Bible through mediation or by tradition. For example, one might learn from St. Paul that certain passages in the Old Testament are to be interpreted Christologically. Or, even prior to exposure to all of the material of the Bible, one might already have the storyline of the Bible in mind because of various experiences in the community of faith. All such knowledge, though mediated, may nonetheless be viewed as the product of what I call "direct reading" or "a pretheoretical grasp of the text."

2. K.J. Popma, "Patristic Evaluation of Culture," in *The Idea of a Christian Philosophy,* ed. K. Bril, et al., (Toronto: Wedge Publishing Foundation, 1973), p. 106.

3. Cf. Hans Frei's view of the concept of identity in narrative as presented in his *The Identity of Jesus: The Hermeneutical Bases of Dogmatic Theology*, (Philadelphia: Fortress Press, 1975). Cf. also a recent, unpublished paper presented in December, 1982, at the American Academy of Religion, in which Frei maintains that the cumulative narrative of Scripture "renders the identity of God." "Theology and the Interpretation of Narrative; Some Hermeneutical Considerations," p. 13. Cf. also G. Lindbeck, "The Bible as Realistic Narrative," *Journal of Ecumenical Studies*, Vol. XVII, No. 1 (Winter, 1980), p. 84.

4. Popma, *Ibid.*, p. 107.

5. The contemporary scholar who has done much to relate the material of the Bible, especially the Old Testament, to a theological grasp of it as integral is Brevard Childs. Though Childs stresses that the canon of Scripture is the canon of the Christian community of faith and is thus a certain use or construal of the biblical material, he also focuses considerable attention on the organization of the biblical material in the final redaction and the significance of that organization for the interpretation of the Old Testament's various parts. Says Childs: "The canonical study of the Old Testament shares an interest in common with several of the newer literary critical methods in its concern to do justice to the integrity of the text itself apart from diachronistic reconstruction." Rather than to recover an original literary or aesthetic unity, however, according to Childs, "The canonical approach is concerned to understand the nature of the theological shape of the text . . . ." *Introduction to the Old Testament as Scripture,* (Philadelphia: Fortress Press, 1979), p. 74. Cf. also, *Biblical Theology in Crisis*, (Philadelphia: Westminster, 1970), p. 99 ff.

6. As Charles Wood has argued in his fine book *The Formation of Christian Understanding: An Essay in Theological Hermeneutics,* (Philadelphia: Westminster, 1981), pp. 118-119: "If the *usus* to be

heeded is that of the writer or first readers of a biblical text, then naturally we who do not share it are obliged to yield to those who, by virtue of their scholarly expertise, can manage to enter into it . . . . Yet, however valuable such an understanding may be to the church, there is a *usus* of scripture which has a prior claim to the church's attention, namely, the *usus* which establishes its canonical sense as God's self-disclosive Word. It is this canonical sense of the text which the church has the most reason to acknowledge as the literal sense of scripture, and that for two reasons. First, it is the theologically prior sense . . . Secondly . . . it is the church's task so to master the canonical sense that it becomes in practice as well as in principle, the measure of the church's own language; only then will the canonical sense function for Christian readers as the 'literal sense' of the text, that is, the natural, obvious meaning as perceived by those who have made its *usus* their own." Confirming this view as essentially also that of the Reformers, Childs remarks: "I am convinced that when the Reformers spoke of the literal sense of the Biblical text as normative (*sensus literalis*) they had in mind the canonical sense and not a hypothetical projection of what scholars thought originally happened." "The Old Testament as Scripture of the Church," *Concordia Theological Monthly*, Vol. XLIII, Number 11, 1972, p. 721.

7.  Cf. Maurice Merleau-Ponty, *Sense and Non-sense,* (Chicago: Northwestern University Press, 1964), p. 52. Cf. also Calvin Schrag, *Radical Reflection*, (West Lafayette, Indiana: Purdue University Press, 1980), pp. 97-127.

8.  Herman Dooyeweerd,*In the Twilight of Western Thought*, (Nutley, New Jersey: The Craig Press, 1975), pp. 6-8.

9.  Adrian van Kaam, *Existential Foundations of Psychology*, (Garden City, New York: Doubleday and Company, Inc. 1969), pp. 45-49.

10. Dooyeweerd, *Ibid.*, p. 8.

11. Gadamer, Hans-Georg, *Truth and Method*, (New York: Seabury, 1975), p. xii.

12. *Ibid.*, p. xiii.

13. *Ibid.*, pp. 5-80.

14. *Ibid.*, pp. 91-114.

15. *Ibid.*, pp. 267-274.

16. *Ibid.*, pp. 239-40.

17. *Ibid.*, p. 246.

18. *Ibid.*, pp. 245 f.

19. *Ibid.*, p. 249.

20. Oden, Thomas, *Agenda for Theology*, (San Francisco: Harper and Row, 1979), pp. xii and 34.

21. Niebuhr, H. Richard, *Christ and Culture*, (New York: Harper and Row, 1956), p. 143.

22. Cf. Lars-Olle Armgard, "Universal and Specifically Christian

Elements in the Writings of K.E. Løgstrup,'' in *Creation and Method: Essays on Christocentric Theology*, ed. Henry Vander Goot, (Washington: University Press of America, 1981), pp. 30, 33-34.

23. Gadamer, *Ibid.*, p. xiv.
24. *Ibid.*, pp. 19-29.

# Notes for Chapter II

1.  Edward Farley, *Ecclesial Man: A Social Phenomenology of Faith and Reality*, (Philadelphia: Fortress Press, 1975), p. 117.
2.  George Lindbeck, "The Bible as Realistic Narrative," *Journal of Ecumenical Studies,* Vol. XVII, No. 1 (Winter, 1980), p. 85.
3.  Hans Frei, *The Eclipse of Biblical Narrative. A Study in 18th and 19th Century Hermeneutics,* (New Haven: Yale University Press, 1974), p. 149.
4.  *Ibid.*, p. 220.
5.  *Ibid.*, p. 1.
6.  Describing Barth's view of the Bible as a whole, David Kelsey says "it is as though Barth took scripture to be one vast, loosely structured non-fictional novel . . ." *The Uses of Scripture in Recent Theology*, (Philadelphia: Fortress Press, 1975), p. 48.
7.  Charles Wood, *The Formation of Christian Understanding: An Essay in Theological Hermeneutics,* (Philadelphia: Westminster Press, 1981), p. 100.
8.  Gustaf Wingren, *Creation and Gospel: The New Situation in European Theology*, (Toronto: Edwin Mellen Press, 1979), pp. 24-25.
9.  In his *The Christian Faith*, (Edinburgh: T & T Clark, 1928), Paragraph 132, Friedrich Schleiermacher describes well the significance of the present arrangement of Testaments in the Bible, though he strongly bemoans the choices made in the canonization process: "The real meaning of the facts would be clearer if the Old Testament followed the New as an appendix, for the present relative position of the two makes the demand, not obscurely, that we must first work our way through the whole of the Old Testament if we are to approach the New by the right avenue."
10. We shall reconsider in Chapter VI how historical criticism upsets the order and structure of biblical narrative as apprehended in the pre-scientific mode of givenness. How difficult it is even for relatively orthodox theologians to take seriously the sequence of biblical narrative as we now have it in the final redaction of the canon is well illustrated by G.E. Wright. According to Wright—I am following his *God Who Acts*, (London: SCM Press, 1952)—our understanding of the canon must begin with the *nation* of Israel and its attempt to explain the events that led to its establishment (p. 44). From the sense of being elect and a special people, Israel inferred a God of grace. From the Lordship of this gracious God Israel in turn inferred the idea that she was a covenant community united to a God of law. Finally, in a last step God's Lordship was extended to all creation (p. 46).

    Now it is interesting to notice here methodologically that the order or sequence of these ideas is not the sequence of their presentation in the canon of Scripture itself. In fact, the dependence of these concepts on one another in the canon runs in exactly the opposite direction from the one that Wright maintains about their relationship. Moreover, this is so because Wright's framework of reference is the historical-critical one, whose baseline is the human—in this case *national*—situation of origin. The Bible itself, however, furnishes us with another framework or perspective, which could be designated the "canonical" one. The baseline of this perspective is the *divine* situation of action, the acts of God in the order in which they address us and thus in the order in which they are depicted in the canon. It is ironic that a theology that stresses the divine sovereignty in history as much as Wright's does should, nonetheless, use a method of analysis that views everything *von unten nach oben* and must thus engage in a reconstruction of the storyline of the Bible that turns its given canonical structure and order upside down.

It cannot be argued either, in my judgment, that these two frameworks—the historical-critical one and the canonical one—are both legitimate in their own right and on their own terms because they are different perspectives on the same thing, each governed by a different set of rules. Since each presupposes a different context of meaning, namely the ontological on the one hand and the epistemological on the other—so the argument goes—the two are not mutually exclusive.

Before we rush to adopt this position of harmonization, it should be asked what in fact it means to say that belief in (knowledge of) God as Creator is a *consequence* of belief in (knowledge of) his Lordship and thus naturally follows it. Is it not thereby being alleged, in defiance of the content of the biblical text as we now have it, that creation-faith was a belief no one could have had in the patriarchal and primeval periods before the formation of the nation of Israel and the emergence of its efforts to understand itself? Leaving aside for the moment the problem of historical criticism's reversal of the canonically given sequence, we might ask whether Wright's historical-critical reconstruction even describes properly the process and steps by which persons in the Old Covenant before the election of Israel came to belief. Creation is clearly canonically first. Should we thus not conclude that it is also therefore logically basic and even historically most original? Nothing really prevents us from saying, e.g., that the patriarchs and persons of the primeval history indeed knew God as Creator. In fact the story as we now have it in the Bible would confirm exactly such an assertion. Belief in God as Creator of the whole cosmos is surely older than the accounts of creation as literary products. Cf. W. Eichrodt, *Theology of the Old Testament*, Vol. II (London: SCM, 1967), p. 97 on the great antiquity of creation faith, which position Eichrodt mentions as running counter to the trend in theological literature.

11.   The exact words here (ποιῶ τὰ ἔϛχατα ὡς τὰ πρῶτα) are credited to the commentary of Hippolytus on Daniel 4:37. Hippolytus claims to

be a follower of Irenaeus. Cf. also Gustaf Wingren, *Creation and Gospel*, (Toronto: Edwin Mellen Press, 1979), p. 36.

12. Besides the view that I take here about the Bible as being essentially a narrative whose non-narrative elements can be related to the narrative elements as commentaries on them, one could also argue quite reasonably that the Bible is a kind of "universal literature." For example, Friedrich Schlegel calls his *Lucinda* a piece of "romantic or universal poetry," intending it to be a potential substitute for the biblical, universal story. By *Roman* or *universal poesie*, Schlegel wished to indicate that this literature represents a combination of all possible forms, that it is a fusion of the greatest variety of literary genres. Moreover, because it is this formally, Schlegel believed that it could present a vast variety of contents also and thus become a comprehensive view of the world in a single book, uniting all the myths. Cf. Hans Eichner, "Friedrich Schlegel's Theory of Romantic Poetry," *PMLA*, 71, 1956, pp. 1018ff.

13. Hans Heinrich Schmid, "Schöpfung, Gerechtigkeit und Heil," *Zeitschrift für Theologie und Kirche,* 70/1, 1973, pp. 3-5.

14. Walter Zimmerli, "The Place and Limit of the Wisdom in the Framework of the Old Testament Theology," in *Studies in Ancient Israelite Wisdom*, ed. by J. Crenshaw, (New York: KTAV Publishing House, Inc., 1976), p. 148. Cf. also Gerhard von Rad, *Wisdom in Israel*, (Nashville and New York: Abingdon Press, 1972), pp. 6 and 60, and Hans-Jurgen Hermisson, "Observations on the Creation Theology in Wisdom," in *Israelite Wisdom: Theological and Literary Essays in Honor of Samuel Terrien*, ed. by J. Gammie, et al. (Missoula, Montana: Scholars Press, 1978), pp. 43-57.

15. Gerald Sheppard, "Canonization: Hearing the Voice of the Same God Through Historically Dissimilar Traditions," *Interpretation*, 36/1 (1982), p. 30.

16. Paul Ricoeur, "Toward a Narrative Theology," unpub. paper presented at Haverford College, Fall, 1982, pp. 15ff.

# Notes for Chapter III

1. For a strong, functionalist statement of this point, cf. especially David Kelsey's *The Uses of Scripture in Recent Theology*, (Philadelphia: Fortress Press, 1975), p. 183.

2. For a good discussion of the complexities of the Catholic view, cf. George Tavard, *Holy Writ and Holy Church*, (New York: Harper and Row, 1960).

3. Kelsey, *Uses*, p. 102.

4. I concur with the following judgment of James Olthuis on this matter as expressed in a recent paper: "Not only is inversion of the creation process a most hazardous undertaking, but historical-critical analysis for all its good has often left us with a dismantled text and no agreed-upon meaning. All these ways can contribute to interpretation, but, in my judgment, the aim of interpretation must center on the subject matter, the what is said of the text. The text must be primarily understood from within itself. The aim is not so-called objective reproduction of authorial meaning behind the text, but the delineation of the author's vision which is fixed in the text, 'in front of' the text as Ricoeur expresses it." "Interpreting an Authoritative Scripture," Institute for Christian Studies, unpub. paper, p. 35.

5. Cf. J.C. Vander Stelt's discussion of this problem under the rubrics of book-religion and secularism in *Philosophy and Scripture: A study in Old Princeton and Westminster Theology*, (Marlton, New Jersey: Mack Publ. Co., 1978), p. 331.

6. This tends to be the view of both classic Thomism and Protestant Scholasticism. Cf. Thomas, *Summa Theologica*, (New York and London: Blackfriars, 1964), Ia, 2,2; and B.B. Warfield, *Revelation and Inspiration*, (New York and London: Oxford University Press, 1927), p. 6.

7. Calvin's famous simile of the Scriptures as *spectacles* expresses well the Bible's instrumental role in knowledge. Cf. *Institutes* I.vi.1 and I.xiv.1.

8. Examples of running the Gnostic risk of viewing redemptive revelation as an alternative to experience, and especially to norm discerning within experience, can be noticed in many thinkers. Elsewhere I have criticized Barth for his "revelational positivism" and its bad consequences for political theory. Cf. Henry Vander Goot, "Creation, Revelation, and Christian Philosophy," in *Creation and Method*, ed. Henry Vander Goot (Washington: University Press of America, 1981), pp. 145-7. Corresponding to Barth is the Anabaptist opposition of the clear revelation of Jesus Christ in the Bible to our sin-stained discernment of norms in creation. For example, John Yoder's "Christocentristic" view of the Bible plays into the tendency to reduce God's revelation to a certain kind of ethical ex-

emplarity perceived in the gospels and symbolized by the cross. Hence there emerges a skeptical attitude toward God's law in creation and our discernment of it and a corresponding well-nigh Gnostic use of the example of Jesus as recorded in the New Testament—as if that story were ever meant to be a substitute for the Christian assignment of norm discernment in God's creation. For a good example of Yoder's method, cf. his *The Politics of Jesus*, (Grand Rapids, Mich.: Eerdmans, 1972).

9. Overagainst the view that the church is a certain grouping of persons with distinctive ideas Gustaf Wingren has argued that the church is the new humanity. For Wingren the church is to be understood primarily on background of creation, not first of all on the background of the gospel so that it becomes viewed as a new system of beliefs and rules. Cf. *Gospel and Church*, (Philadelphia: Fortress Press, 1964), pp. 3-11; and *Flight from Creation*, (Minneapolis: Augsburg Press, 1971), p. 15.

10. For the inappropriateness of applying a relational or dialogical view of truth to the relationship between Scripture and its reader, cf. E. Schuurman, "Gods Openbaring en menselijk denken," *Beweging 81*, 45e jaargang no. 3, juni 1981, pp. 42-3. This article is a critical review of *God Met Ons*, a 1980 report on the nature of scriptural authority of the Gereformeerde Kerken in the Netherlands. Cf. also what Walter Lindemann says about Barth's view of the biblical text as subject in *Karl Barth und die Kritische Schriftauslegung*, (Hamburg: Evangelischer Verlag, 1973), p. 18.

11. Gustaf Wingren, *The Living Word*, (Philadelphia: Muhlenberg Press, 1960), p. 42.

12. Dietrich Bonhoeffer, *Act and Being*, (London: Collins, 1962), p. 15.

13. *Ibid.*, p. 16.

14. Kornelis Miskotte, *When the Gods are Silent*, (New York and Evanston: Harper & Row, 1967), p. 15.

15. Cf. G. Ebeling, *Kirchengeschichte als Geschichte der Auslegung der Heiligen Schrift*, (Tübingen: Mohr, 1947), pp. 22f.

16. Cf. Calvin's view of the work of the Spirit in connection with Scripture, whose Word, according to Calvin, he confirms and establishes in our hearts. *Institutes* I.ix.

17. Speaking of Calvin's own relationship to Scripture, R.R. Niebuhr describes well how the Bible forms its believing reader: "The most direct way in which to characterize Calvin's theology is to say, again, that one puts the matter of Calvin's relation to the Bible askew, if one represents him as merely being subservient to Scripture as a heteronomous authority or as a catena of theses. Instead, it seems to be the case that Scripture authors Calvin, that is, it enlarges him. It becomes his vocabulary, his house, his eye, and his imagination. It is, therefore, far more than a book; it is a chorus: of histories, prophecies, psalms, and visions. It is these which have

come to live in the 'author,' and he in turn endeavors to establish them in the hearts of his readers." "The Tent of Heaven," *The Alumni Bulletin* (Harvard Divinity School), p. 20.

18. Though Schleiermacher speaks only of the impression left on man by God's universal revelation in the world, he does describe the mark that it leaves in terms of the notion of feeling or felt-wholeness. Cf. *On Religion: addresses in response to its cultural critics,* (Richmond, Virginia: John Knox Press, 1969), pp. 84-90.

19. Jonathan Edwards, "Religious Affections," in *Jonathan Edwards,* (New York: Hill and Wang, 1962), pp. 206-227.

20. Herman Dooyeweerd, *In the Twilight of Western Thought,* (Philadelphia: Presbyterian and Reformed Publ. Co., 1960), pp. 145-6.

# Notes for Chapter IV

1. which appeared in the *Journal of Religion* (1961), pp. 194-205.
2. which appeared in *Theology Today*, 37 (1980), pp. 27-38.
3. (Philadelphia: The Westminster Press, 1970)
4. (St. Louis: Concordia Publishing House, 1977)
5. Brevard Childs, "The Old Testament as Scripture of the Church," *Concordia Theological Monthly*, Vol. XLIII, December, 1972, p. 710.
6. Paul Ricoeur, *Interpretation Theory: Discourse and the Surplus of Meaning*, (Fort Worth: Texas Christian University Press, 1976), p. 92.
7. Brevard Childs, "The Sensus Literalis of Scripture: An Ancient and Modern Problem," in *Beiträge zur Altestamentlichen Theologie. Fest. für W. Zimmerli zum 70. Geburtstag*, ed. H. Donner, (Göttingen: Vd. hoeck and Ruprecht, 1977), p. 93.
8. Wood, Charles, *The Formation of Christian Understanding. An Essay in Theological Hermeneutics*, (Philadelphia: Westminster Press, 1981), p. 40.
9. *Ibid.*, p. 119.
10. Erich Auerbach, *Mimesis: The Representation of Reality in Western Literature*, (Princeton: Princeton University Press, 1969); and Hans Frei, *The Eclipse of Biblical Narrative: A Study in Eighteenth and Nineteenth Century Hermeneutics,* (New Haven and London: Yale University Press, 1974).
11. Frei, *Eclipse*, p. 1.
12. Erich Auerbach, "Figura," *Scenes from the Drama of European Literature*, (New York: Meridian Books, 1959), pp. 58-59.
13. Auerbach, *Mimesis*, pp. 14-15.
14. *Ibid.*, p. 160.
15. Frei, *Eclipse*, p. 76.
16. *Ibid.*, pp. 78-79.
17. *Ibid.*, p. 89.
18. *Ibid.*, p. 129.
19. *Ibid.*, p. 127.
20. *Ibid.*, p. 90.
21. *Ibid.*, p. 152.
22. *Ibid.*, p. 130.
23. Wingren, *Theology in Conflict*, (Edinburgh: Oliver and Boyd, 1958), 167-8.
24. Cf. Friedrich Schleiermacher, *Hermeneutik. Nach den Handschriften neu herausgegeben von H. Kimmerle*, (Heidelberg: Carl Winter, 1959). Cf. also for a good discussion of Schleiermacher's theory, Frei, *Eclipse*, chapter 15.
25. Rudolf Bultmann, "Zum Problem der Entmythologisierung," *Kerygma und Mythos 2: Diskussionen und Stimmen zum Problem*

*der Entmythologisierung,* ed. Hans-Werner Bartsch, (Hamburg-Volksdorf: Herbert Reich, 1952), p. 207.

26.    Franz Overbeck, *Über die Christlichkeit unserer heutigen Theologie,* (Leipzig: Fritzsch, 2nd edition, 1903), p. 25.

27.    Joachim Kahl, *The Misery of Christianity: A Plea for a Humanity Without God,* (Middlesex: Penguin Books, 1971).

28.    *Ibid.,* p. 111.

29.    *Ibid.,* p. 121.

30.    *Ibid.,* p. 112.

31.    *Ibid.,* p. 156.

32.    *Ibid.,* p. 161.

## Notes for Chapter V

1. Among the Reformers a significant difference is present between Luther and Calvin in the area of hermeneutics. While Luther tends to stress the kerygma *in* the two testaments and the fact that generally the Old stands under the rubric of the law and the New under the rubric of the gospel, Calvin is more focussed on the Bible as canon. For Luther the Word is in the Bible; for Calvin the Word is the Bible as a whole. Thus, it is natural that Calvin would stress the similarity of Old and New in II.x. of the *Institutes* as much as he does, viewing the differences merely as forms of presentation and not as substantial.

2. D.J.A. Clines says of the word "theme" that it is "deeper" than the word "plot" or "subject matter." To discern a theme is "to see 'the attitude, the opinion, the insight *about* the subject that is revealed through a particular handling of it.' " "Theme in Genesis 1-11," *The Catholic Biblical Quarterly*, Vol. 38 (1976), p. 485.

3. By speaking of the "essence" of Christianity, I do not mean to accept the terms of the 19th century debate about it. However, I do wish to relate to that debate, but I shall view "essence" not as something *behind* the text, or even as some *idea* within it, but as the overall *structure* of the text itself. I have thus appropriated approvingly a combination of Herman Dooyeweerd's religious notion of the "fundamental motive" of biblical revelation, *Roots of Western Culture: Pagan, Secular, and Christian Options*, (Toronto: Wedge Publ. Foundation, 1979), p. 9, and Anders Nygren's more aesthetically oriented notion of the "fundamental motif" of Christianity in *Agape and Eros*, (Philadelphia: Westminster Press, 1953), p. 42. Needless to say, I do not associate myself with Nygren's specific, and I think reductionist, view of that fundamental motif as being the New Testament notion of *agape*.

4. Robert Alter, *The Art of Biblical Narrative*, (New York: Basic Books, Inc., 1981), p. 156.

5. This point is actually taken from Hans Frei's description of what realistic narrative is. Cf. his *Identity of Jesus Christ: The Hermeneutical Bases of Dogmatic Theology*, (Philadelphia: Fortress Press, 1975), p. xiv.

6. Cf. J.V. Langmead Casserley, *The Christian in Philosophy*, (New York: Charles Scribner's Sons, 1951), pp. 244-45.

7. For a good sense of this in Scripture, cf. M. Van't Veer's model study of the Elijah-Ahab story in *My God is Yahweh: Elijah and Ahab in an Age of Apostasy*, (St. Catharines: Paideia Press, 1980).

8. Clines, *Ibid.*, says in his interesting article that "When chapter 1 (of Genesis) is also taken into consideration, some case can be made out for 'creation-uncreation-re-creation.' " p. 500.

9. John Herman Randall, Jr., *The Career of Philosophy, Vol. I*, (New

York and London: Columbia University Press, 1962), pp. 383 and 385. Cf. also Herman Dooyeweerd, *A New Critique of Theoretical Thought,* Vol. III, (Philadelphia and Amsterdam: Presbyterian and Reformed, and H.J. Paris, 1957), pp. 18-20.

10.   E.A. Burtt, *The Metaphysical Foundations of Modern Science,* (Garden City, N.Y.: Doubleday and Co., 1954), pp. 52, 67, and 238-9.

11.   Cf. the structure of Barth's *Church Dogmatics,* which argues that the essential biblical pattern is eternal election in Jesus Christ and the temporal reconciliation of God and man. Accordingly, Barth not only argues an epistemological Christocentrism, but also grounds this approach in a corresponding ontological Christocentrism.

12.   This pattern is evident especially in the philosophy of Hegel and in theologians—such as Wolfhart Pannenberg and Jürgen Moltmann —that express Hegelian thought in Christian terms.

13.   Working with 19th and 20th century conceptions of what is real and what is possible, critics of the direct reading of the biblical text berate it by calling it "naive," "realistic," "objectifying," and "mythological." This attitude comes to extreme expression in such noted theologians as Rudolf Bultmann and Gerhard Ebeling, who embark upon radical programs of "demythologization" and "deobjectification" to uncover the "real" meaning of the Bible. Cf. Bultmann, "The New Testament and Mythology," in *Kerygma and Myth,* ed. H.W. Bartsch, (New York: Harper and Row, 1961), pp. 3-6. According to Ebeling, since modern man thinks in terms of scientific and historical categories, the "realism" of biblical images cannot be accepted. Because of the Bible's naive conception of reality, its language must become the object of historical criticism, which abolishes it and renders the message intelligible. *Dogmatik des christlichen Glaubens* II, (Tübingen: Mohr, 1979), pp. 372, 374, and 395.

14.   Oscar Cullmann, *The Earliest Christian Confessions,* (London: SCM, 1943), p. 38.

15.   For this argument I am indebted to Gustaf Wingren, *Creation and Law,* (Edinburgh: Oliver and Boyd, Ltd., 1961), pp. 5-7.

16.   One of the weaknesses of Hans Frei's view of the Bible as realistic narrative is his almost exclusive focus in Scripture on persons, actions, events, and their interrelationships. It is indeed the case, as Frei argues convincingly, that the Bible reveals the identity of God and that this identity emerges most pre-eminently in the person of Jesus Christ. But scant attention is paid to the *product* of the divine action in creation and what this reveals about the divine identity. In Frei's narrative theology, history—the unfolding action—bears all the burden of revelation. Accordingly, Frei tends to ignore the non-narrative. He relentlessly stresses that actions must be rendered and represented in the terms of the actions themselves. Moreover, he

also focuses almost exclusively on narratives *within* the Bible as compared to the Bible as a single narrative. Hence, Frei tends to miss the movement *in the Bible itself* from person and event to *commentary* and to the development of general principles of intelligibility. One might wonder here whether Frei's Wittgensteinen inclinations do not blind him to the cosmological aspect of the Bible and thus to the thrust toward universality and the cosmic focus that is so much a part of the Bible's own orientation toward creation in particular.

17. Walter Eichrodt, *Theology of the Old Testament*, Vol. II, (Philadelphia: Westminster Press, 1967), pp. 98-99.

18. Cf. here in particular Georges Florovsky, *Creation and Redemption*, (Belmont, MA.: Nordland Publishing Co., 1976), pp. 51-62. Florovsky distinguishes carefully between what is of God's intra-trinitarian essence and nature and what is of God's extra-trinitarian will. For Florovsky, hence, the intra-trinitarian relationship of begetting or generation that exists between the Father and the Son is a wholly inappropriate analogy for the extra-trinitarian relation that exists between God as such and creation. Cf. also chapter 10 of Book XI of Augustine's *City of God*.

19. According to biblical religion, though the world is not-god, it is nonetheless not appearance either, but real in its own terms. For a more elaborate discussion of this view of the status of creation, cf. Langdon Gilkey, *Maker of Heaven and Earth*, (Garden City: New York: Doubleday and Co., Inc., 1959), pp. 60-1.

20. Though Augustine underestimates evil by viewing it as a privation in his sustained attack on Manicheanism, one distinct advantage of his use of Neo-platonism at this point is his refusal to admit that any "natural reality is evil." *City of God*, Book XI, chapter 22 and Book XII, chapter 1.

21. One of the major arguments of Gerrit Berkouwer's large volume on the doctrine of sin is to insist that it is impossible to explain sin in terms of the circumstances that surround it. According to Berkouwer, the biblical view interests us in no factors "other than our guilt." *Sin*, (Grand Rapids, Mich.: Eerdmans, 1971), p. 19. Cf. also Augustine, *City of God*, Book XII, chapter 6.

22. Calvin, *Institutes*, II.i.9.

23. Nygren, *Ibid.*, pp. 46-48.

24. Attacks on the legal conception of the atonement, such as that of Gustaf Aulén in his famous *Christus Victor*, really rest on structureless views of creation as a fluid order, ostensibly to accommodate more adequately the idea of divine sovereignty.

25. Douglas Schuurman, "Creation, Eschaton and Ethics: An analysis of Theology and Ethics: An analysis of Theology and Ethics in Jürgen Moltmann and an Alternative proposal," unpub. paper, University of Chicago Divinity School Doctoral Seminar, August, 1982, p. 44.

# Notes for Chapter VI

1. Cf. Edward Farley, *Ecclesial Man: A Social Phenomenology of Faith and Reality*, (Philadelphia: Fortress Press, 1975), pp. 8, 51, 55, 50, 78, and 232.

2. *Waarom zou ik naar de kerk gaan?*, (Nijkerk, The Netherlands: Gallenbach, 1971), p. 78.

3. "Patristic Evaluation of Culture," in *The Idea of a Christian Philosophy*, ed. K. Brill, et al., (Toronto: Wedge Publishing Foundation, 1973), p. 107.

4. This appears to be the "solution" towards which Wood tends in his book *The Formation of Christian Understanding*, (Philadelphia: Westminster Press, 1981), p. 89.

5. Cf. in this connection Gerhard Maier's claim that critical method has "withdrawn reason from claims to revelation." *The End of the Historical-Critical Method*, (St. Louis: Concordia Publishing House, 1974), p. 23.

6. Klaus Scholder, *Ursprünge und Probleme der Bibelkritik im 17. Jahrhundert. Ein Beitrag zur Entstehung der historisch-kritischen Theologie*, (München: Chr. Kaiser Verlag, 1966), pp. 8-9.

7. Hendrikus Berkhof, *Christian Faith: An Introduction to the Study of the Faith,* (Grand Rapids, Mich.: Eerdmans, 1979).

8. Henry Vander Goot, Review of *Christian Faith* by Hendrikus Berkhof, *Calvin Theological Journal*, Vol. 16, No. 2, Nov. 1981, p. 233.

9. Berkhof, *Ibid.*, p. 166.

10. Berkhof, *Ibid.*, p. 167.

11. On the matter of alternative myths or stories present in the categories of critical scholarship, cf. Jean Starobinski, "Criticism and Authority," *Daedalus*, Fall, 1977, p. 14: "(The) triumph of the *analytical mind (esprit d'examen)* went hand in hand with the appeasement of religious conflicts and with the end of antagonism between rival theological dogmatisms. Reinforced by this victory, critical knowledge was soon to elaborate its own myth and to turn this into a substitute dogma: historical scholarship . . . is one of the aspects of the progress of reason, at the end of which humanity, conciliated and divinized, will enter into the great unitary realm of achieved Science."

12. Langdon Gilkey, "Cosmology, Ontology, and the Travail of Biblical Language," *Journal of Religion*, Vol XLI, July 1961, No. 3, p. 203.

13. For an excellent recent example of such an attempt at "Umdeutung," cf. Jürgen Moltmann's *The Future of Creation*, (Philadelphia: Fortress Press, 1979). In the naive attitude of thought, creation is what happened in the beginning. Creation is the first chapter of the biblical story and the reader of the Bible must

make his way through that story first properly to grasp the meaning of the subsequent action, which comes to be seen as the *re*storation of creation. But for Moltmann salvation and justification cannot be a *re*storation of man springing from the beginning. The "Future of Creation" is not the restitution of a paradise lost but the eventual coming into being of the first perfect creation, which never yet has been (pp. 169-70). The "Future of Creation" means the creation that will be in the future, not the destiny of the creation that has already existed for a long time, from the beginning. Moltmann does not seem to worry about the fact that there is no sense in which the depiction and structure of the biblical narrative as we now have it leaves that impression. Better then to say what the narrative depicts and disagree with it than to present as its *real* meaning a view that in effect turns the whole narrative from creation to consummation right around.

# Name Index

# Subject Index